How to Keep Your Child from Going to JAIL

Forever Families,

Forever Blessing

Hubert Gaines

2010

What Others Are Saying About How to Keep Your Child From Going to Jail

This book is a must read for all parents, guardians, and anyone contemplating rearing children. He has taken the time to let us see what happens when parents drop the ball with our children. Amen to the chapter on giving children a spiritual foundation and bringing it home with the home rules for each age category.

Lorene Brown Watkins, National Vice-President, Ameri-Plan Corp, Dallas, Texas

After more than twenty years on the bench, and many thousands of life-altering decisions, Judge Hubert L. Grimes speaks with unquestioned authority and conviction about the challenges facing today's youngsters and their parents. In How to Keep Your Child from Going to Jail, Judge Grimes offers parents sound, practical, and heartfelt advice on how to divert young people from delinquent behavior and keep them on the road to success.

Gordon Johnson, President, Neighbor to Family, Inc., Daytona Beach, Fla.

I believe this book should be read by every parent and pastor. There are churches on almost every corner of our cities, yet we have problems with our young adults going to jail. Scriptures say, "My people perish for lack of knowledge." This book will aid parents and leaders in helping our youth to fulfill their destiny in life. This book is very timely in this season when parents are having to get two and three jobs to make ends meet, leaving the children to train themselves. I thank God for giving Judge Grimes a heart to help our youth.

Dr. David Rosier, Pastor, Fellowship Church of Praise, Panama City, Fla.

How to Keep Your Child from Going to JAIL

Restoring Parental Authority and Developing Successful Youth

The Honorable Hubert L. Grimes

iUniverse, Inc.
New York   Bloomington

How to Keep Your Child from Going to Jail
Restoring Parental Authority and Developing Successful Youth

Unless otherwise indicated, all scripture quotations are taken from the King James Version of the Bible.

iUniverse books may be ordered through booksellers or by contacting:

iUniverse
1663 Liberty Drive
Bloomington, IN 47403
www.iuniverse.com
1-800-Authors (1-800-288-4677)

ISBN: 978-1-4502-0539-9 (sc)
ISBN: 978-1-4502-0541-2 (dj)
ISBN: 978-1-4502-0540-5 (ebk)

Printed in the United States of America

iUniverse rev. date: 02/18/2010

Commemoration

This book honors the life and service of our nephew, First Sergeant Michael S. Curry. Michael, a twenty-year veteran paratrooper with the 173rd Airborne Division of the United States Army was killed by a roadside bomb in July 2006 while serving in the southern region of Afghanistan. We celebrate his life, sacrifice, and the sacrifice of the thousands of young men and women who are risking their lives to ensure our freedom. A portion of the book sales will be donated to the Smiles are Contagious Foundation set up in his honor to provide mentoring programs for youth. View the work of the foundation at www.smilesarecontagious.org.

Contents

Foreword

As parents, grandparents, guardians, schoolteachers, neighbors, and friends, we often pause, after the fact, and wonder what steps, if they had been taken, would have been life-altering for our children. Our central concern is to aggressively pursue preventive measures to arrest negative behavior and to promote freedom and holistic living—not incarceration—for our offspring.

Once a child enters the juvenile justice or criminal justice systems, many unexpected things can occur. There can be a quagmire of competing essentials that envelop children once they are on the inside. They may become more defiant, glued to an established or emerging behavior that does not favor a wholesome attitude or negates an existence as a contributing citizen of the society. Children once vital, vibrant, and engaged can become introverted and isolated from family and friends, and others who genuinely care.

Children find themselves in trouble with their parents, schoolteachers, law enforcement, and ultimately, the court system. Mistakenly, children think that they have the answers for what is best for them now and in the future. They don't. Simply put, too many children have been and are incarcerated. The numbers are too big to ignore.

There is enough blame to go around as to what has gone wrong with this generation. Many parents have decided to be pals and not parents; teachers have struggled to get the message across that students have the responsibility to go into class to find the meaning of the lesson and not to lessen the meaning of the assignment. What was once considered as children just going through a stage of rebellion, often develops into a pattern of bad girls and bad boys propelling themselves toward, drugs, alcoholism, gang violence, failure in school, and yes, incarceration.

Increasingly, we express disbelief in the bodacious, in-your-face, "last word" approach of this youthful generation. They have a broad range of conduct that embodies a courageous disrespect and blatant unwillingness to follow directions, accept instructions, or live a life that focuses on tomorrow, not just the immediacy of today. Moreover, we wonder who should have been responsible for a generation in which too many think they deserve a standing ovation for just having arrived at the schoolhouse door.

There are also numerous juveniles who have material pleasures not because they earned them, but because their parents spoiled them with creature comforts. They have been allowed to concentrate on things, not thoughts. Parents wonder why their child is not excelling in school. They seek to cast blame on others, often ignoring the fingers that are pointing back at them. They want positive results from their child's educational journey, but are often unwilling to acknowledge what they should have or could have done to enrich the child's upbringing.

This distinguished jurist, professor of law, and author, Hon. Hubert L. Grimes, has seen and heard it all. As he sits on the bench, he faces those who as a result of their misdeeds are fractured, fragmented, and sometimes frail. Pleas for mercy are uttered by parents, family members, children, and sometimes even victims or their families. Their child is in trouble and their lives have been disrupted. He is the arbiter of justice, not for some, but for all. He has the burden of deciding their plight for the betterment of the child defendant and society.

Let the record be clear, there is a difference in just thinking that you would do one thing in a given situation and actually being engaged in the decision-making and problem-solving that shapes and molds a child's life. This author's educational training, excellence in achievement, longevity, and commendable experience on the judicial bench match his ability and compassion for humankind. This combination causes him to listen and hear the allegations and facts as the legal arguments are placed into evidence so that he can decide what is best for the person who stands before him.

Hindsight is 20-20. Now, we are afforded invaluable insight as to what can and should be done before a child reaches a crisis stage. In these pages, we learn tangible skills, doable best practices, and practical strategies that, if followed, will literally save this and future generations of our children from jail and ensure their successful future. I highly recommend that you consider his astute insights and practical recommendations.

Patricia Russell-McCloud, J.D.
President, Russell-McCloud & Associates
International Motivational Speaker,
Atlanta, Ga.

Acknowledgments

First and foremost, I give thanks to God for the opportunities and life experiences that form the foundation for this book project. This book is dedicated to the loving memory of my parents, the late Robert and Welthie Grimes. They kept me on the straight and narrow path during the critical formative years of my life. They instilled the values in me that carried me through the challenges of youth, college, career, and even the raising of my own family. It is to my parents, who symbolize the tenacity of the generations past, and to the generations to come that this labor of love is dedicated.

To my loving wife, Daisy, I am humbled by your support, inspiration, and your giving spirit that have touched my life and the lives of numerous young people as we seek to live the life we talk about in front of our children and others. To my daughter and son, Ebun and Jamal, whose choices in growing up have made the lessons in this book real. To my daughters by marriage, Tammy and Tiffany, I honor you for being willing to create a seamless, blended family. Each of you coalesced as sisters and brothers and has made me proud for the love you share for one another and your mental toughness to succeed in your chosen fields of endeavor. To our grandchildren, Brittany, Brandon, and

Eric, you are each messages that are being sent to a future that will be created by your words and deeds. To my nieces, nephews, god-children and protégées, I am grateful for your allowing me to infuse you with many of the nuggets of wisdom contained in this work.

While I am indebted to many teachers and coaches throughout my life, two individuals are of special recognition. I will be forever indebted to my godmother, Euphemia "Momma" Reeves, who guided my spiritual growth and development. Equally as important to my life and career is Attorney Pat Russell McCloud, my mentor and the person who motivated me to pursue law school. She has continued to counsel me through various stages of my career and graciously took time out of her international travel schedule to produce an inspiring foreword for this book. In addition, I am grateful for my trusted and dedicated judicial assistant, Belinda McElveen, who has given loyal and dedicated support for over twenty years. Thanks to Dr. George Bradley, who encouraged me with the words, "Get it wrote and then get it right." I am appreciative of both my adopted sister, Dr. Carol St. James, and my daily prayer partner, Renell Smith, for their continuous encouragement. A special thanks to my daughter-friend, Dr. Michelle Thompson, who helped me with editing and encouraged me during our mutual adventures in writing, and to her cousin and my fraternity brother, Marvin Emmons, for photography and cover design. I extend my appreciation to the following persons whose assistance made this book project possible: Gloria S. Brown and Joan Thompson, for their secretarial assistance; Dr. Willie Kimmons, for showing by example how to produce a quality book that impacts the lives of people; and Dr. Winona Fletcher, my ever-present college professor who continues to inspire, correct, and challenge me to this day, who provided preliminary editing of this manuscript. I am also indebted to Attorney Ruby McZier and Judge Dawn Fields for their ideas and editorial assistance. To my sister Judy, who quietly works to keep the Grimes family intact, as well as my siblings, Obi, Robert, and Wendell, I love and appreciate each of you. I also am thankful for my extended family, Jackie, Marjorie, Luther, Steve, and Sandra whose support and nurturing have been a dynamic part of my personal growth, and for Pastor Jim Raley, who challenges me to move into a new spiritual dimension. To my court staff in general, and Deputies Jose and Christy in particular, who reviewed the manuscript and gave me excellent feedback, thank you. To the countless others who have influenced my life, directly and indirectly, I give thanks to God for each of you. Let us continue to work for the improvement of the next generation.

Introduction

Every day, parents find themselves astonished when they are
confronted by the unbelievable reality that their child has been
arrested and is now standing before a judge facing prosecution,
maybe even jail, for crimes committed. These parents have many
questions running through their minds. How did this happen?
What did I do wrong? Is my child going to jail? How long is
he going to be away from me? What will my family think of
me? How could I have failed? What will my friends say about
me? How am I going to make it without my son or without my
daughter? What's going to happen to my baby? Will my child get
hurt behind bars?

The family is the primary unit for the transmittal of any
culture. Even though twenty-first century America has become
a diverse society, there are common threads of right and wrong
that exist among us all. Whether one's ethnicity is white, black,
Hispanic, Asian, Caribbean, or other, each parent desires to see
his or her child succeed in life. Yet to succeed in America, it is
critical for our young people to do well in school. Often the very
strength of our country—its diversity—creates challenges in
schools where educators struggle with balancing academics and
acceptable behavior. In times past, when a child's behavior got

out of control, the schools were able to redirect the youth through admonishment, detention, or a call to the parent. Today, more and more youth who engage in misconduct end up in front of a judge. Whether the misconduct is an isolated act of one youth stealing another student's cell phone or iPod, or a fight between rival gangs in the school cafeteria, such crimes often cause the perpetrators to end up in front of a juvenile court judge.

The schools are caught in a tremendous struggle. They struggle to promote academic achievement against a backdrop of out-of-control student behaviors. The quest for ever-increasing test scores often comes into direct conflict with youth who want to impress gang leaders or those who are educationally challenged and labeled ADD, ADHD, ODD, or a host of other medical conditions. In times past, children were sent to school with the expectation that the school would fix whatever was wrong with them. Today, public schools, which are increasingly diverse culturally, racially, and economically, find themselves struggling with the same issues as society in general, coupled with an increasing acceptance of mediocrity. It is not unusual, particularly in the inner-city schools, to find teachers and administrators becoming increasingly frustrated as they seek to bridge the various divides in an effort to produce students whose mission is to make the world a better place for us all. Parental support is an essential element in helping to mold student expectation with performance. That is true no matter the culture, the race, the gender, or the language spoken by the parent or student.

Often, the court system becomes a dumping ground for students who fail to conform to expected conduct in school or who choose to violate the laws by which we all are expected to be accountable. One of the most emotionally driven moments in the life of a parent is to witness his or her son or daughter being led into custody by a police officer. Put behind bars or sent away to a commitment program, the child is ordered to a place where his or her freedom is no more. It is a place where the corrections staff determines the time that one wakes up or goes to bed. Bathroom use is not a matter of personal convenience; it is a matter of permission. Food choices are no longer as simple as going to the kitchen in the middle of the night to raid the refrigerator. The breakfast, lunch, and dinner meals are not based on standards of fine dining or the melodious jingle of advertised specials imploring you to "have it your way."

The detainees do not have it their way in food choices or anything else. They have swapped their personal freedoms for the momentary rush that occurred during the commission of the criminal or delinquent act. It is no longer about what one likes, it is about doing the time for the crime. It is about changing the behavior that put the individual in jail in the first place. It is about handling the length of time, the distance from loved ones, and the restraint of one's freedom in order to get through the jail sentence. It is about the changes that are needed to make sure that the child does not become a repeat offender whose destiny, if it remains unchanged, will result in a collision course with state prison when the youth turns eighteen, or sooner if certain adult-type crimes are committed. Through all of this experience, the parents are asking themselves the questions: "How did my child get to this place? What did I do wrong? This is not supposed to happen to me, only to other people."

This book is designed to shed some light on the growing problems of juvenile delinquency and provide guidance to parents experiencing the challenging responsibility of raising their children into adulthood. I also hope that many parents will avoid the bitter desperation that occurs when kids cross the line and end up behind bars. While there is no guarantee in this world except death, taxes, and eternity, the intent of this book is to share some time-tested revelations, which, if implemented, will increase the chances of achieving family happiness and stability and keep your child out of jail. Use them to help you, your child, and your community. Let's work together to keep your child out of jail and help him or her build a successful future.

Chapter One:

How This Book Came About

As a judge, I took an oath to uphold the law and work to improve the administration of justice. Over my years of service, I have witnessed thousands of young people come through the court system charged with delinquent acts. While I continually work from the fundamental principle of the child's best interests, all too often my work is too little, too late. The damage has already been done, and many of our youth have already adopted a mindset that will ultimately lead them on an irreversible journey to state prison.

Many of the attitudes that triggered these delinquent acts could have been changed if parents had recognized the long-term consequences for their failure to establish proper limits during the formative years of the child's development. While there will always be a small percentage of those who in spite of strong parental controls still stray into negative behavior, the vast majority of young people desire loving parental limits. In this book, I will share practical tips that upon proper application will steer kids away from delinquent behavior and onto the path of success. In the process, our collective efforts will reduce the number of youth who are dropping out of school and getting caught up in the criminal justice system.

My Journey

My personal journey started in the small town of Bartow, Florida. During my youth, Bartow, like many other southern communities, was a segregated town. While segregation caused whites and blacks to live apart, many of their core family values were similar. I know this because my mother spent almost as much time helping to care for and raise the doctor's children who lived across town as she did in raising us. Although we were from different sides of the tracks, all of us were taught to respect adults, to share, and to follow the norms of that day. In spite of the fact that my mother was their maid, she was respected by the doctor's children.

On many occasions, Momma was asked by the doctor's wife to talk to the kids and get them back in line. Later, when our two segregated schools merged into one integrated school, the doctor's daughter and I ended up taking several classes together. His son, two years my junior also took Spanish class with me. We were always friendly toward one another and just recently we reunited via e-mail. We, as with many of our other classmates and friends, have found out that the basic core values of love, honor, respect for elders, and hard work that were developed during our youth, continue to be passed down to our children and grandchildren, irrespective of our different racial backgrounds.

Although my parents were limited in their education, they were not limited in their values. My dad finished sixth grade and my mother completed a night school diploma program only a few years before I graduated from high school. Both had stopped attending school while growing up in order to help their families, but my mother never gave up on her dream of a high school education. She often worked two jobs, and she made hats and sewed clothes as a sideline. Dad also worked hard jobs by day and often side jobs in his spare time. They believed in God, family, hard work, discipline, respect, obedience, church, giving to others, never giving up, and the true spirit of love. Values such as these are not limited by color, language, or gender. These same values must be reinforced to our youth today, without regard to race, gender, or language. These are the same core values that allow young men and women to come together in the military and fight for our country's freedom without regard to race, gender, language, or geography. These values represent the key to our country's future.

Long before I began my tenure as a judge, the framework for my life was created by parents who expected their children to be obedient, do well in school, obey the law, go to church, and be nice to people. As a child growing up, my life's experiences were molded by parents, teachers, coaches, and an extended community network. I still don't know how I could throw a rock at a stop sign on one side of town and have my mother know about it before I got home. And that was long before cell phones existed. There was little, if any, mischief that I could get away with while growing up because every adult considered his or herself to be my surrogate parent with the right to correct my conduct and report to my mother what I had done. This usually resulted in a second admonition. And if I denied the allegations, it meant I was calling the adult a liar and the admonition now became punishment.

My mother kept me busy with activities at school and with church and community events. Boy Scouts, Tiger's Lair Club, Junior Police, choir practice, sandlot football, tennis, and being an athletic trainer left little time for foolishness. Each activity played a role in developing responsibility and shaping my personality.

Against the template of my early life, I bring to bear the experiences of being a trial judge. I have adjudicated over one hundred thousand cases, ranging from traffic citations, accidents involving injuries or death, misdemeanors, drugs and alcohol, sexual misconduct, domestic violence, small claims, civil lawsuits, injunctions, extraditions, felony crimes, domestic relations, juvenile delinquency, abuse, neglect and abandonment of children, termination of parental rights, adoptions, child support, paternity, and a host of others. For the last ten years, my focus has been drawn to family law cases—particularly parent and children issues, ranging from crimes of abuse and neglect, to drugs and abandonment.

Over the years, I have learned that there are certain truths in raising children to become productive adults. This book is designed to provide advice that I believe will assist willing parents through the journey of raising their children and creating a wholesome family. I pray that all of my readers will be blessed by what they read and implement from this labor of love.

Chapter Two:

How Did We Get Here?

O n any given day in family court, it is highly likely that I will deal with kids who have attacked or physically hurt their parents and even grandparents. In one such instance, two sisters, ages ten and twelve, who were adopted at the ages of two and four by a single mom with years of experience in working with troubled children, began to terrorize her and destroy the contents of her home. The oldest daughter continually stayed out past curfew, putting herself into dangerous situations by walking or hitchhiking from one small town to another during the darkness of the night.

At times, she and her sister destroyed household furnishings, including a computer, a television, bedroom doors, and windows, for no other reason than they got mad for being told to stay in the room as punishment for misbehaving. On another occasion, the older child concocted a tale that she had been raped by an adult male who had befriended her. After spending several months in jail, the man was exonerated by a jury when her story unraveled and DNA results turned out to be negative.

These were not bad kids at first. They were kids who started out in life sweet and kind. Both had received all of the perks that a caring, adoptive parent could muster. You could even say that they were spoiled, always getting the best of everything that their adoptive mother and new family could provide, including televisions and computers in their bed-

> *Many parents spoil their children with every material toy available, but never give them the things they truly need such as love, discipline, and encouragement.*

room, designer label clothing, the latest gadget toys, and collectible dolls. But somewhere in the process of getting the material gifts, something was missing. Something caused these adorable children to become holy terrors.

Their story is not unlike many others that I have witnessed and been called upon for solutions. Many parents give their children everything they can buy and fully believe that doing so will cause the children to love and respect them. Unfortunately, it doesn't always work out that way. Sometimes, the kids take such parental kindness for weakness. And, as in the instance with the two adopted sisters, negative conduct moves beyond the limits to the point where criminal or delinquent conduct occurs, necessitating law enforcement and judicial intervention.

One day I reviewed the case of a recovering drug mother who just had her sixth child from the fourth different father, with no idea as to the identity of this baby's daddy and doubts about the paternity of the others. A few cases later, there was a nineteen-year-old mother of two children, whose high school dream was to become a medical doctor. But after getting involved with the wrong guy, she started partying, doing drugs, and not long after, got pregnant—not once, but twice. After two babies, she found herself alone. Her dreams were crushed, and she now stood alone, abandoned by her baby's daddy. His lifestyle was heavily influenced by the street life of fast money, drugs, "bling-bling" jewelry, and fancy, juiced-up cars. She was drawn to him because of the image he perpetrated. But that same guy left her after the birth of the second child. She became homeless and lost custody of her children and all hope and expectation that she could ever be anything other than a failure. Her self-esteem was destroyed, and the stress of her life caused her to look much older than her true age. He had called her "his woman," but he had abandoned both her and their children.

By the afternoon docket, a fifteen-year-old girl appeared in front of me who had been released from custody and given an opportunity to attend teen court to resolve the delinquency charges of battery against her mother. Unfortunately, the tables had turned and she had become the object of her mother's scorn. When the daughter politely asked the mother to drop her off at the courthouse to attend the teen court session, the mother went into a tirade and cursed the daughter. "What makes you think that you are so good? You think you are better than I am?" The mother's anger toward the child in this case was not because of the child's behavior. Instead, the child had become the scapegoat for the mother's stress, the result of an ailing husband, money problems, work issues, loneliness, and more. In her frustration, she forced the child out of the car and made her walk the rest of the way to the courthouse, without regard to the dangers of the street and further demanded that she find somewhere else to stay.

While the above cases are factually unique, they represent just a small sampling of the thousands of kids, who have issues and for whom, without parental intervention, the judicial system becomes their destination. Some youth are in custody for burglarizing cars and houses, while others are there for possessing or selling drugs, committing domestic violence against parents or girlfriends, grand theft auto, gang activity, weapons, shootings, or the like. Shoplifting is minor when compared to these crimes. Other children have been abandoned by their parents because of drugs, domestic violence, or other parental failures.

Not all of the cases involve criminal acts against others. For example, it has been necessary to remove newborn babies from young mothers when they tested positive for heroin, cocaine, or marijuana at birth. In one such case, when I asked the name of the infant's father, the young mother, who had dropped out of high school after getting caught up in a lifestyle of partying, drinking, and drugging, was unable to identify the baby's daddy from the fifteen to twenty guys she slept with around the time of conception. Such was the result of a lifestyle of drugs, partying, and a major lack of self-esteem.

While the names are withheld, the stories are true and are a mere snapshot of the myriad of struggles that confront many of our youth today. No concerned parent wants to believe that their precious little one could end up in the negative situations described throughout the course of this book. The hope is that these facts will open the eyes of parents and children alike and reduce the negative consequences that result from irresponsibility, a lack of self-discipline, and disrespect for others, whether caused by parent or child.

In spite of the emotional challenges of each day, I remain confident there are many among this large sea of humanity who can and will turn their lives around. On some days, the task is to find a stable home for a three-year-old kid with a big, beautiful smile and bouncy personality who has been abandoned by parents on a drug binge. On other days, I find myself reuniting a family after the parents have gotten their lives on track and no longer require the oversight of the court system.

While today's news headlines often focus largely upon the failures of government and corporate America and how they abuse taxes or profits to dominate people, there are many people whose personal lives mirror difficult challenges on a smaller scale. They seek to dominate people—some are successful, others are not. Yet many times, it is painfully obvious that the negative behavior is transgenerational. Kids, having grown up in negative environments, end up duplicating the conduct of parents and sometimes grandparents. They learn based on what they experience or witness. In the process, many take on the learned behavior of domestic violence as the best way to solve their problems. Their motto becomes "If you can't persuade them, just beat the crap out of them. And if you need some help to get it done, then my cousin, the gangsta will certainly be glad to help you out."

This book is not merely about reciting the stories of family court. Instead, the intent is to offer guidance to parents on how to keep their children from ending up behind bars while building strong, loving, and prosperous families. The goal of the book is to encourage parents to raise responsible kids who enjoy a life of learning, growing, and serving their community, while keeping children away from the negative conduct that will result in confinement. Throughout the course of this book, I will share insights and wisdom gained from twenty-plus years on the trial bench and my interaction and involvement with numerous young people. I have also sought to tap into the wisdom and commonsense principles and traditions that were instrumental in my own life—rearing of my own children who have grown into successful, productive adults and working with the multitudes of young people that have passed through my courtroom, classroom, or who have been mentored by me.

A Sample Letter from a Troubled Youth
July 10, 2009

Dear Honorable Judge Grimes,

Here I am once again standing in front of you for the charge of possession. I know it was wrong having cannabis on school grounds. As a matter of fact it was wrong having it all. You have to try and understand why I use it. The only reason and time I'll use it is when I'm angry or upset because it calms me down and keeps me relaxed and I'm usually under the influence when I'm at my house because it's crazy in there.

Words don't even explain the commotion that goes on through the household. My mom's still trying to commit suicide. The last time she tried was almost 2 months [ago] and she overdosed on a lot of pills. And she's always taking up when her and my dad fight, like the other day they were fighting really bad and I kept hearing things hit the walls and a lot of yelling and then my mom takes off in the car, nearly hitting my dad speeding down our road at least 60 miles an hour in a 35 mile zone and my dad gets in the car and chases after her. And my dad always accuses me of taking everything that comes up missing. I do admit some of the things I normally have but then again, I don't have some of the things and he's way too quick to judge. And my brother's girlfriend that's 21 threatened to kill me because I got on her about not watching her kids and she tried to hit me and she's pregnant, and 21. She actually left a scratch on my neck but it's gone now.

My brother is like the only person I get along with in our household. It's stressful and crazy. It really is and that's just the short version. If you only knew how things were at my home you would probably understand me a little better. And about two weeks ago 5 of my friends got into a horrible car accident off of Kepler. One of them had to be flown to Halifax Medical Center to get brain surgery and stitch his ear. Another one broke his spleen, collarbone, back and is in concussion and a full body cast for 3 months, and the rest of them had cuts and bruises and probably sore. But that had me really upset and nervous but they're all okay now so that's good.

Now I'm gonna (sp) talk about school, it's been great for me. I've already gotten a credit, brought one of my Fs to a C and my GPA is higher, being at school is the only place I feel good about myself because I see the progress I'm making and it feels really good. I've never been more proud of myself, but I just wanted to tell you how things have been. Thank you

Sincerely,
Susie

[Author's note: The contents of this letter are real; the name was changed to protect the child's identity. Errors in spelling and grammar were intentionally left as submitted by youth.]

Chapter Three:

Becoming a Parent Means Plenty of Sacrifice

Having children and raising children are two different matters. While the age for having children seems to be decreasing in our society with younger teens having babies, there is a corresponding increase in the challenge of raising children who are respectful, productive, and positive. While many husbands and wives are choosing to delay having children until later in their relationships when careers and finances are better established, adolescents and teens are continuing to become pregnant, sometimes as young as ten or eleven years old.

> *Giving birth to a child is one thing, but the parental sacrifices to raise a child require greater determination and effort.*

Many of these "babies having babies" are clueless as to the essential elements of raising children. I have dealt with at least three young females who gave birth prior to age twelve.

Their unprotected sexual conduct resulted in an unexpected pregnancy. After having a child, many teen parents return to their previous practices, except now they have the added responsibility of caring for and raising a child. Without the guidance of parents, grandparents, or other mature relatives, children often end up raising themselves, while getting their influences from television, videos, music, and the influences of others who are their same age or maturity. Many of these children are more naive than they realize and often believe what they see in the media, striving to emulate that conduct.

Many teen mothers continue to deal with the same issues after giving birth as they did before they got pregnant. Often the result is a duplication of their mother's similar pregnancy when she was a teen. Remarkably, the conduct repeats itself, generation after generation. Some of these young ladies will actually admit that they set out to get pregnant because they believed the baby would give them someone to love and be loved by. These young ladies are not sure that they will get the same love from their baby's father or for that matter from their own parents. Many of their parents are tied up in their own world of drugs, partying, and the nightlife, or for that matter, jail, often leaving these girls to raise themselves. The teen mother often thinks the baby will be a fitting substitute for the love and attention she has failed to receive from her parents, family members, or boyfriend. Too many teen parents end up that way only because they are looking for love in the wrong places.

While there are numerous "surprise" pregnancies among both married and unmarried adult couples, the manner of handling these matters can be totally different. For married couples, nine out of ten times the surprise pregnancy is a welcome one that they had hoped for, either to begin or expand their family. Even if not expected, most married adult parents make the adjustment and welcome the newborn into the family with joy and laughter.

On the other hand, when pregnancy occurs to an unmarried couple, the range of emotions varies depending on many factors—whether the couples are adults, the length of the relationship, the extent of their commitment to each other, moral values, financial ability, job, cultural heritage, etc. For those who are less than the accepted national legal age of eighteen and living at home with their parents, the news of an unwanted pregnancy is even more life-changing. Plans for the prom or homecoming dance must now take a backseat to having and raising a child. College and career options are often deferred or cancelled outright. All too often, the teen mother is left holding the baby and the diaper bag as the immature teen father goes on about his business—playing sports, music, or picking up a new girlfriend who doesn't have the baggage of the baby.

Once the teen mother finds out that the baby's daddy has a new girlfriend, the "baby momma drama" starts. The teen mother, who is caring for the child, goes over to the teen daddy's house for what appears to be the twentieth time in a week to tell him that the baby needs diapers and formula—except the real reason for the visit is not to get the needs of the baby met, it is to interfere with the so-called new relationship. And, of course, if the new girlfriend is present, a real Jerry Springer drama erupts with name calling, yelling, and even fighting.

During a hearing on a petition for restraining order against violence, I learned that two young women, who were both dating the same guy, got into a physical fight in one of the local teen nightclubs. After giving them a chance to vent their rage toward each other, I asked how long each had been dating "Mr. Don Juan." One stated that she had been with him for two years, while the other stated that she had been with him for four years. I asked if either of them intended to break up with him and they both vehemently stated "No." I then asked, "So why are you fighting with one another? You both know about each other, and neither of you intends to stop dating this young man, and obviously, he intends to keep both of you on a string. Why don't you share him? Each of you can have him for three days out of the week, and he can have one day off." They both looked at me as if I were the crazy one. I dismissed the petition and sent them away. Don Juan, the lover boy, was not in court that day as he was probably busy with girlfriend number three. I have not heard from either of them again, so some arrangement must have been worked out.

The lesson to be learned is this: when a baby is born, the needs of the child outweigh the desires and conveniences of the parents. Whether talking about the physical needs of food, clothing, and shelter or the emotional needs of love, affection, holding, and comforting, parental conveniences must give way to the well-being of the child.

Many school districts offer special accommodations to teen parents and their babies. However, the parents of these teenagers are certainly not off the hook. Even though parents may be disappointed that their daughter got pregnant or their son has fathered a child out of wedlock, it does not change the reality that a newborn will be arriving soon and everyone's life will be changing.

To avoid the same pregnancy situation and subsequent drama occurring again, parents, grandparents, and extended family must come together to help raise this new addition to the human race. Choosing to be a parent is far easier than being a parent. Whether the choice is made by a mature adult or by a teenager for all the wrong reasons, becoming a parent is not an easy or short-term event. The primary focus shifts from the desires of the parent to the needs of the child. Child-rearing is certainly not for the fainthearted—nor is it a temporary encounter. It is a journey that will last a lifetime and requires maturity. Be prepared.

When teens choose to become parents, their lives immediately change. The challenges faced by mature adult parents are greatly exacerbated in the life of teen parents. For example, adult parents adjust their work schedules, rearrange their priorities, and pay for child care and babysitters. They literally reframe their lives around the needs of the newborn child, even sacrificing participation in social activities when necessary. Teen parenting requires even more sacrifice. Teen parents often want a more normal teenage lifestyle, like their non-parent peers. Teen parents are usually not as mature when it comes to giving up the homecoming dance, the football or basketball game, prom, or other social events. Weekend events such as movies, dances, and other social outings become more difficult to attend because of the challenge of obtaining child care, particularly where limited funds are available. When the child is sick, the teen misses school or causes another relative to miss work.

Long before a parent has to deal with their child's teen pregnancy, there are some strategies that can help steer kids away from the premarital sexual conduct that precedes the pregnancy. The most important strategy is parental supervision. Know where your child is at all times and with whom he or she is spending time. One of the most critical periods when mischief occurs with teens, is the window that occurs from the time school lets out for the day until parents get home from work. Statistics that are discussed later in this book show that a significant amount of juvenile crime occurs during this time period. I would venture to say that many teen pregnancies also occur during this same window of opportunity. Adult supervision, whether parental or through school-based activities, will minimize the opportunity for such misconduct.

Communication is critical. As kids are growing up, it is important for parents to create a nonjudgmental atmosphere with their children. This will encourage them to talk about the things going on in their lives and in the lives of the young people with whom they associate. The building of the child's self-esteem is a critical element to establishing good parental communication. Self-esteem is one of the best defenses against teen pregnancy. A child who feels good about him or herself does not require additional validation from others. Parents must set standards and values that establish acceptable conduct. Structured adult-supervised activities, such as sports or community or church youth groups, reinforce positive values and keep kids busy so that their idle, unsupervised time is minimized.

School-based sex education, though helpful, is not enough. Parents must never be afraid to discuss the topic of sex with their children. They are exposed to sexual innuendo, marketing, music, and suggestiveness every day of their lives through media, television, video, and peer conversations. Never assume that because parents are not talking to children about the subject, that they are not receiving information from other sources, even if it comes from those whose knowledge is as factually limited as your child's. The oft used slogan of "just say no" to sex or drugs is not enough. Kids who are left without adult supervision may become bored and may use sex like some kids play sports. Know the whereabouts of your children and who they are with in order to protect them from impermissible conduct.

But merely telling children that you expect them to act a certain way, without reinforcement, is not enough. Kids are very smart and if there is any degree of hypocrisy in their parent's conduct, children who want to exploit the situation will attempt to do so. It will take parents and extended family to help children get through the various phases of their lives, particularly during the teenage years. Each of the suggestions that follow, and more, are elaborated upon in the chapters to come.

Practical Tips

1. The decision to become a parent means putting the needs of the newborn child above the desires of the mother or father.

2. The party life must take a backseat to caring for a child, not only until the baby is born, but throughout the life of the child.

3. Teen parenting adds additional and challenging issues for all parties involved.

4. Parents who lead their children by example have a greater chance of helping their children successfully through the minefields and pitfalls of the teen years.

Chapter Four:

Give the Child a Spiritual Foundation

Train up a child in the way he should go and when he is old, he will not depart from it. Proverbs 22:4 Holy Bible (KJV)

I n reviewing hundreds of background reports used for sentencing recommendations, I remain amazed that a large majority of the juveniles that I deal with are disconnected from any form of faith-based experience. A significant pattern emerges from the reports, commonly stated as, "child does not attend church and is not involved in any structured community activity." Seeing this phrase in the predisposition report often raises a red flag, allowing me to conclude that the child has not been regularly exposed to core moral or spiritual values. Such youth create their own standards of right and wrong, which are often based on selfishness, greed, and arrogance.

In the absence of a strong spiritual foundation, the child is left to follow the ideas of peers, television and music, or in the alternative the code of the Wild, Wild West: do bad to others before they do bad to you. Such dog-eat-dog values can only result in a society of anarchy. Nobel Peace Prize recipient and noted civil rights leader, Dr. Martin Luther King, often reminded America that "to follow the Hammurabi code of an eye for an eye and a tooth for a tooth will eventually leave us all blind and toothless."

The key to building strong moral values in children begins with teaching positive spiritual values from the earliest days of a child's life. Such values should include, but are not limited to, faith in God, respect for parents and persons in authority, treating others as one desires to be treated, and love and respect for oneself and others. These essential values are the building blocks in the framework of human dignity.

Every child is trained from the womb by the influences of parents and those to whom they are exposed. Parents must be mindful that children develop 90 percent of their personality from birth to adolescence. During this time, children are sponges that absorb everything around them, whether those things are good or bad. If a child is exposed to lots of smiles and laughter, it stands to reason that he or she will develop a happy persona. If parents use a lot of profanity around the child, in all likelihood he or she will do the same. Dr. Erik Erickson, noted psychologist, in his discussion on personality development stated: "From age six to puberty, children begin to develop a sense of pride in their accomplishments. They initiate projects, see them through to completion, and feel good about what they have achieved. During this time, teachers play an increased role in the child's development. If children are encouraged and their initiatives reinforced, they begin to feel confident in their ability to achieve goals. If initiative is not encouraged, if it is restricted by parents or teachers, then the child begins to feel inferior, doubting his or her own abilities and perhaps not reaching his or her potential."

Therefore, it stands to reason that the biggest influence in a child's life is that of the parents. Parents who want to raise positive, productive children into adulthood must be aware of the things to which their children are exposed. You are the greatest influencer of the success for your child. Take a look at yourself and guard the future of your child through the personal standards that you set and live by.

My Own Spiritual Journey

While sitting as a Florida trial judge for over twenty years, I maintain my humility by reminding myself that by traditional thinking, I am one of the least likely persons to be where I am. Although my parents had limited schooling and worked hard for a living, they pushed each of their children to get a good education. While education was very important in our family, a critical element of my success and that of my brothers and sisters has been our spiritual foundation, which was created by my parents in general and my mother in particular.

From as far back as I can remember, my siblings and I were required to attend church. The core values of love for God, family, and the care and concern for others, became second nature. In combining the values of a spiritual foundation with the love for education, family, and community service, three of five siblings completed college, one completed secretarial school and has worked in the school system for over thirty years, and one has worked as a truck driver for over fifteen years. All of us have been able to care for ourselves, our families, and successfully raise our children to do the same. I attribute their success stories, and particularly my own, to the spiritual foundation we received, thus enabling each of us to build successful careers. In carrying out my judicial duties, I regularly seek God's wisdom in helping to make the difficult decisions, particularly as it relates to addressing family and children issues. I believe that a strong spiritual foundation lies at the core of human success, whether it is acknowledged or not.

As a child growing up it was expected that everybody would attend church. Sunday school, church service, choir practice, or the host of other related church activities that were a frequent and essential part of our childhood. As a teenager, I had to attend church even if I stayed out late on Saturday night, whether the event was school-related or a party. The work of the church in my life created a value system that clearly distinguished right from wrong. It instilled confidence and a servant leadership attitude that came about long before the phrase became popular.

While I can never claim I did not have some failures in conduct in my childhood, when I look back they were minor bubbles that were as the whisper of a passing storm cloud. On the other hand, we are now experiencing a generation that is being continually peppered with media images on television, videos, and in music that often tear down, rather than build up, standards of respect and righteousness. Often, God's commandment, "thou shall not kill" is being replaced with a mindset that teaches kill or be killed, and to make sure that you kill, "do it with a drive-by."

On several occasions in my life, people I knew or went to school with made choices that resulted in serious consequences. Some made decisions that were stupid, which resulted in getting kicked out of school; others were reckless in their driving habits and ended up being injured or killed. Still others made decisions that were actually criminal and resulted in long-term jail sentences. In at least two instances, death was the ultimate consequence. I look back over my own life and am continually reminded that there but for the grace of God, go I.

Changing Values, Changing Results

We are witnessing a cultural upheaval that threatens not just traditional values, but the value of life itself. Video games have become an indispensable part of teenage life. Kids kill avengers in their video world, who are resurrected to be killed again. The line between fantasy and reality becomes blurred. Couple that with the desensitivity that results from drug use or repeated viewing of violent images, and one has a recipe for destruction, be it theft, murder, or other forms of mayhem.

The antidote for this behavior and the conduct that leads to it must be found in the home-based values to which our children are exposed. Children are like sponges; they pick up the teachings to which they are exposed. Whether it is the bumping gyration of the most recent dance moves or the values of a Sunday school education, children learn and emulate the things that they see and come into contact with.

My time on the bench has made it painfully obvious that many of our youth have little, if any, respect for authority. The disrespect exhibited in court (until they are challenged) or on the street toward police officers or with teachers at school, often pales in comparison to what is going on in the home. Peeping behind the veil of the home, it often becomes obvious that children are duplicating much of the behavior to which they have been exposed. A childhood filled with cursing, fighting, and drugging on the one hand, or the complete absence of parental controls on the other, will result in blatant misconduct once the adolescent years arrive.

Even more painful are the children of tender ages such as the eight- to ten-year-olds who erupt into rages against their parents or teachers. Unfortunately, I hear too many parents say, "I can't do anything with him." Recently, my office was contacted by a mother who wanted me to talk with her son who she stated was out of control in the home. On numerous occasions, at the request of parents, I have met with kids prior to their being thrust into the court system and the discussions have borne fruit. Yet the situation surrounding this particular request was truly extreme, as the mother advised my assistant that the youngster with whom the mother had lost control was the ripe old age of six years old. To me, the child is not the problem, but the parent.

The relinquishing of parental control did not happen overnight. Parental surrender often begins in the diaper stages and continues through the tantrums and public exhibitions without consequences. It ends up being displayed to schoolteachers, to law enforcement, and sometimes to the court until there is a dose of "steel bar" therapy.

I was blessed to have my parents until they were eighty and eighty-seven years old respectively. Throughout their lives, until their passing in 2002, I respected and honored them both. I attribute that respect to the spiritual values and influence instilled in me by my parents from the time of my birth through childhood into adulthood and even until today. They believed the God given directions of Proverbs 22:6 that they should "train up a child in the way he should go and when he is old he will not depart from it." They also applied the biblical instruction of Proverbs 13:24 to not "spare the rod and spoil the child."

Children will absorb what they are taught. The Ten Commandments, as outlined in Exodus 20, require us to give respect to God, honor our father and mother, not kill, steal, lie, or be jealous of one's neighbor or his possessions, etc., are not outdated values. Regular attendance at churches, synagogues, or temples that emphasize child-based teachings is a great place to start, particularly when parents are also involved. Parents who also practice what they preach have a greater impact on the lives of their children, than those who are hypocritical. In fact, parents who tell kids to "do as I say and not as I do" are fooling themselves. They are actually teaching kids to be hypocrites who will do one thing in their parent's presence but act very different elsewhere. When confronted, they will say, "I only act the way I was taught." This is not the result most parents expect, but it is the consequence of conduct which developed over a significant period of time.

Downward Spiral of Values

In a society that has come to emphasize money, power, and sex as the virtues of life, is it any wonder our children are operating with little or no restraint? We are living in the most blessed country on the planet, during the most prosperous period in history, even in spite of the recent economic downturn. Technology has brought about conveniences that tend to make us think that our success is the result of our birthright and we can have whatever we want if the price is right. We throw away people like empty food wrappers with little concern for the damage caused to people or the environment. As a result, we often forget that the blessings of our lives are not an entitlement, but the result of grace.

Too many baby boomer parents have removed their own personal restraints as a result of the free-loving sixties, the soulful seventies, the I-got-mine eighties, and the we-have-arrived nineties. Too many parents don't have time for God anymore because they are either busy making it to the top of their careers or enjoying the fruits of their labor. Things like going to church, family prayer, delayed gratification, or the golden rule that tells us to "do unto others the way we would desire them to do unto us" have become outdated or of minor importance.

Our courts, which helped to open doors of opportunity for millions including disparate groups of women, the disabled, and people of color, also removed the time-honored tradition of prayer from public schools. Unfortunately, over the last forty years we have also witnessed further changes: declining respect for authority in schools, increasing violence, and lowering of the value of an education. Educators push fervently to educate the minds, but often miss the hearts of children. Therefore, as a society, we have continued down a slippery slope, fearful of involving the foundational principles of the Ten Commandments or Jesus' admonition to love thy neighbor as thyself. We began and continue to intersperse situational ethics as part of a curriculum of tolerance—but unfortunately, many times, tolerance for the wrong conduct.

Our society is becoming fond of making the weird seem like the norm. The behavior that would have once caused classmates to ostracize or rebuke a child is now embraced as being cool. God has been booted out of school, homes, and sometimes, even the church. He has been replaced at school by situational ethics, a philosophy of doing what you feel is right under the circumstances or what you feel is good for you without respect for its impact on others. He has been replaced in many homes by the television wars of HBO, MTV, BET, and VH1. The virtual reality of video games such as *Kill Master*, *Grand Theft Auto*, and other criminal enterprises exposes too many of our youth to blurred lines between fantasy and reality. Some youth even attempt to duplicate what they see in the video world as part of gang initiations, even if the victims are real. Then they brag about their conquests on MySpace, Facebook, Twitter, and other social media, including chat rooms.

God has even been booted out of some churches. Many attend but do not want to conform their lifestyle to the time honored values of God's Word. Some people believe that God is not politically correct because He does not condone the sins of the flesh, while others refuse to embrace or understand the power of forgiveness. We are left with shells of church buildings, and many attendees go through the motions of attending church but leave the services unchanged. Is it any wonder that with the absence of major spiritual influences, we are being left to our own devices? We are now seeing a generation of youth who seem to be focused on self-destruction and a lack of caring for anyone else, be they parents, siblings, friends, or strangers. We have modeled a world, scripted by weird imaginations, which is causing more of our youth to end up behind bars. They have little hope for tomorrow, or worse, are dying from drugs, violence, or sheer disconnectedness.

Solutions Begin in the Home

Many people blame the school system that no longer allows prayer as the reason our societal values are breaking down. While I am sure the absence of prayer in school has had an impact, even more important is the absence of prayer in the home. Further, prayer should never be ritualistic for the sake of prayer alone. The kids must witness the parent living a life that is consistent with the spiritual beliefs being proffered. What are some of these core values? Love for self and one another as family is a great place to start. Personal unselfishness and an environment of peace in the home, free of arguing, cussing, criticizing, or domestic violence is next. Finally, positive encouragement and building of self-esteem at home will carry over into school and other areas such as sports, music, and art.

During a church school summer program in which my wife was teaching, she reminded parents in attendance to be careful what they say around children and never go home after church and gossip about people on the telephone. As soon as the words came out of her mouth, a small hand shot up in the back of the class and a six-year-old child yelled out, "Ms. Grimes, Ms. Grimes, my momma doesn't wait until she gets home to talk about people on the phone. She talks about people in the church parking lot." Need we be reminded further that children indeed are always watching and listening to what parents are doing? It is important that parents teach, preach, and live the values that they want their children to emulate. Children learn from the things to which they are exposed. There already exists too much negativity in the world. Far greater efforts must occur at home in order to balance the scales.

Changing the Spiritual Landscape

The prescription for curing many of the problems with our children is this: parents must change before their children will change. Parents must take the role of establishing a spiritual foundation for their homes. Where they have been prior failures, acknowledge them to yourself first, and start from where you are to get it right. Find a church that teaches the word of God and regularly attend with your kids. If they do not want to go, take them anyway. The earlier this new life starts the better.

Pray together. Let them see you pray and get them involved with the prayers. It will bless their lives long after they grow up. Start living what your new life teaches. If changes need to be made in your current situation, make them. Your destiny and your children are more important than the current conveniences. From my own experience, I am convinced that God is well able to guide you beyond the loss of any creature comforts. Read and study the Bible. Teach kids. A good place to start is a daily dose of Proverbs. As you regain control of your spiritual and home life, you will begin to see a change in your kids. Don't be a hypocrite. Where kids are older, even teens, don't expect positive changes to occur overnight. Yours did not. But keep the focus and the new life. The breakthrough will happen. It is just a matter of time. Do not let the craziness of this world steal your children. Pray for their daily protection, and see God move on your behalf. Live the life you profess and eventually your child will get on board.

Practical Tips

1. Regain control of your spiritual and home life.

2. Read and study the Bible with your child.

3. Teach kids the time-tested values such as those found in the Book of Proverbs, the Beatitudes of Jesus, and the Gospels.

4. Pray for the daily protection of your children.

5. Live by example the things that you teach.

Chapter Five:

Talk to, Not at Your Kids

> *Parents who argue or scream at their kids continuously will trigger self-esteem issues in the children, which may later manifest in destructive behavior.*

Communication with your kids is one of the most important tools available to parents. Newborns start out with the unintelligible goo-goo, gaga of baby talk. Many parents start out reading to their child while he or she is still growing in the womb. As the child grows and develops, the words may change, but the parental purpose remains the same: to create an environment that will foster mutual understanding, expectations, positive development, independence, and interdependence.

Unfortunately, many parents have lost the art of communication with their children. Instead, they holler and scream at the top of their voice and some even go to the point of using profanity toward their children. When children grow up in a profanity-laced household, there is a strong likelihood they will emulate the behavior. While some will curse in the presence of their parents, others will do so only when the parents are not around. On the other hand, some will become introverted because they are criticized and cursed at for everything so much that they end up lacking self-esteem.

Renowned commentator, Olivia Kay, writes in a recent article, "Why Verbal Abuse Can Be Just as Damaging as Physical Abuse" that although, "bruises can usually be seen on the body of someone who is physically abused, no bruises appear on someone who is abused verbally or emotionally. However, stinging words and personality attacks can do more damage emotionally to a person than one generally realizes." Verbal abuse of a child can lead to a lack of self-esteem. Lack of self-esteem in children often leads to destructive behavior. The behavior can manifest itself in self-destructive harm such as cutting one's self, drugging, or delinquent conduct against others. When a child is constantly being put down by the same parent(s) that he or she looks up to, the resulting effect is traumatic. The kids who are subjected to such negativity may:

- Develop a mindset that says, "I will never be good enough to please my parent(s)."

- Internalize the idea that "my birth must have been a mistake for them to talk to me like they do."

- Be persuaded that their parent(s) don't love them.

- Become convinced that their negative friends accept them when their parents don't—even believing this group is their real family that will back them up in times of challenge.

- Think that it is okay to do drugs, since the worst thing that can happen is to overdose and die since their parents don't care about them anyway.

- Develop anger toward their siblings, believing that their parents must love the sister or brother more because they don't get yelled or cursed at.

- Think that they might as well cut themselves or take pills to end the misery, at least that way they won't have to hear the cussing and put downs anymore.

> *Nine out of ten times, a child will not run away from loving, caring, and nurturing parents unless there are other issues in the home.*

Many parents wish to take back words they have spoken to their children, but often such attitude is too little, too late. The child who is ostracized or unfairly criticized may often leave home, join a gang, commit delinquent or criminal acts, and end up in jail, prison, or dead. Children are told in Proverbs 13:24 to "obey your parents in all things." But love and respect is not one-sided. Parents are told in Proverbs 22:6 "to not provoke your children to anger, lest they be discouraged." Love works best when it is reciprocal between parents and children.

Communicate with your children. Speak in a tone that is conversational. Meaningful dialogue between parents and children helps children gain confidence in their relationship with their parents. Talking to a child does not mean giving the child control of the conversation. Remember, you are a parent first and not their friend or pal. There will be plenty of time after the child grows into adulthood for the relationship to evolve into friendship. While they are children, you are a parent first.

Talk with your children about their day. Ask how many new friends they made that day at kindergarten, school, etc. Did they do anything fun? Was lunch good? What new thing did they learn today? Establishing a pattern of discussion with a child early on will make it easier to talk with the child during the difficult transitions of adolescence and teenage years.

Yelling and screaming at your children is not an effective way to parent. Why? No one hears you when you are yelling, especially not the kids. There may be moments to yell, such as to protect them from danger, but daily yelling and screaming creates insecure or dogmatic children—neither of which are good in the long run.

Practical Tips

1. The conversations we invest in our children carry long-term impacts. Make them positive.

2. Consistent loud screaming and hollering at a child does more harm than good.

3. Build trust in your children by listening when they speak.

4. You are a parent first, not a friend or buddy to your child.

Chapter Six:

Who's in Charge of Your House?

From the time that children can verbalize their desires, whether through crying or words, they begin the "I want that" syndrome. Often parents will give in to the whims of children to placate them. While for an infant it may be another bottle, or a piece of candy or a toy for a toddler, as they grow older the cry doesn't change, but the object of their desire does. When left unchecked, the temper tantrum of a child screaming and falling on the floor of a grocery or department store because he is denied a candy bar or other sugary treat escalates into other demanding, or even worse, intimidating acts toward the parent. As an unchecked child gets older, such out-of-control behavior pushes the envelope and often the child ends up standing in front of a judge facing delinquency charges.

> *Learning to say no to a child at the right time is an act of love.*

In our courtrooms today, there are numerous examples of teen and even preteens who have physically attacked their parents. Many of these girls and boys started out being permitted to talk back to their parents in a disrespectful manner. Calling parents by their first names instead of mom or dad, cursing at them, threatening or punching them, hitting, and even pulling knives or guns on their parents are just a few of the numerous out-of-control actions that I have addressed in open court. Often, there are many other acts that go unreported because the parents are intimidated by teens who are larger in physical size. Other parents are embarrassed to acknowledge that their children are out of control.

While many vivid examples come to mind, a glowing contrast occurred in court recently. A mother appearing with her fourteen-year-old son was asked by me if she could control her son at home. The answer would assist me in knowing whether I could trust the child to follow my court order as he was being released from custody. Her response was startling; she replied, "Look at him, he's bigger than me, I can't control him or make him do anything." Several cases later, I asked the same question of another mother appearing with her son who was about the same age and size. The response was quite different. That mother stared back at me, and rolled her neck and head while replying, "What do you mean, can I control him at home? Absolutely, I handle my house and this kid, too. It's only when he leaves home and hangs out with those other idiots that he gets in trouble." To which I noticed the second kid drop his shoulders and hang his head in anticipation of the dressing down he was going to get at home from his mother, merely because the judge had even asked such a question. The first kid on the contrary smirked as if to say, "I know she can't control me and I will do what I want to do."

Both boys were about fourteen or fifteen years of age, and both stood taller and bigger than their mothers. However, one mother was intimidated by the physical size of her son, while the other mom was not. The second youth has not returned to court for any more trouble, while the parent who announced the fear of her son in his presence has been back multiple times and that child has been put in custody repeatedly, finally being committed to a lengthy juvenile program.

Two problems are identified by this scenario. First, the fear of the child did not start out in the courtroom, but long before. When a child is permitted to disrespect a parent or adult figure, absent some intervention, the child will continue to do so. The child will push the envelope until he or she crosses the threshold of violence toward a parent. Yet the intimidation is not limited to the parent. Once the child subconsciously realizes that he or she can get what he wants from another person by intimidation, the actions will not stop until someone forces it to stop. What started as a tiny snowball during Lil Johnny's infancy because the parent refused to tell the child no, soon develops into a full-fledged avalanche by the time Lil Johnny reaches the teen years. Saying no is more an act of love than letting Lil Johnny always have his way.

Loving a child doesn't always mean saying yes. More often, love can and must be expressed by a parent learning when and how to say no, and the sooner, the better. Love is knowing when and how to say no to your children. When necessary, love requires disciplining your children. Many parents have actually told me in court that it is against the law to spank one's children. Such a statement is far from the truth. It is against the law to abuse one's child. But Florida law and the laws in many other states, now specifically provide that corporal discipline of a child by a parent or guardian for disciplinary purposes does not in itself constitute abuse when it does not result in harm to the child. [*Florida Statutes* 984.03(2)]

While one might not be surprised that parents and teens struggle in their roles as noted above, it is beyond comprehension to see such conduct with younger children. I was shocked recently when my assistant shared an interesting phone call she had received earlier in the day. A mother called our office seeking help with a child that she described as out of control. Over the years, I have counseled with numerous youth in an effort to keep them out of the system. I usually invite the parents to bring them to court to observe the proceedings as a wake-up call. This particular mother stated she couldn't do anything with the child as he was completely out of control, terrorizing her and destroying things in the house. Not an unusual situation, that is, until she told my assistant that the child was six years old. Certainly, the parent, as well as the child, needed a wake-up call. God forbid if a six-year-old is terrorizing the house, what will occur when he is sixteen? Parents, it is your God given right and responsibility to raise your children and not let them control you.

Practical Tips

1. Parents have a duty and responsibility to control their children and not allow the children to run the household.

2. When parents do not set limits for children at home, children will carry that disrespect for authority to school and into their dealings with other adults, including law enforcement.

3. Children function better in an environment where they know what to expect and there is loving discipline in the household.

Chapter Seven:

Spend Time with Your Kids

P arents who grew up amid limited resources often want to give their children the material things that they did not have. Many parents work two jobs and sometimes three, in order to give their kids designer clothes, jewelry, sneakers, or the latest technological gadgets. Often parents give children too much in the way of material things, but do not know how to impose limits on those same children. Many of these kids become spoiled brats and develop an attitude of entitlement and ungratefulness toward the very parents who are continually sacrificing for them. Yet many parents will not stop the madness of continuing to give to these spoiled brats. Instead, they complain and continue to give. The child's attitude of entitlement becomes exponentially worse, until the disrespect for parental sacrifices carries beyond the home into the school and community. Sooner or later, the breaking point occurs. The child is arrested for committing a delinquent act, and as a result, both the child and the parent get wake-up calls.

Your story does not have to end like this scenario. Parents, wake up! Overindulging kids with material things is a surefire way to create problems. The antidote for parents is to start while children are young. Love and discipline, more than material things, will teach respect, build character, and maintain consistency in conduct.

> *Time spent with children is a wise investment for the parent and the youth.*

Modern American society is the picture of run-run, faster-faster, more-more. Many of us have too much on our "to do" list. In fact, recent statistics suggest that in the average two-parent American family, parents spend less than twenty minutes of quality time on a daily basis with their children. Yet according to a 2007 report compiled by the United States Census Bureau, "parents are taking a more active role in the lives of their children than they did in a similar study conducted ten years ago." The census data is based upon a comparison of time spent in 1994 to similar information examined in 2004. The survey combined the time spent by parents with children talking at the breakfast table, talking when the children arrive home from school, parental supervised playtime, dinnertime, and preparing for bedtime. The irony is that the total amount of time reported, as limited as it is, still represents more than the 1994 survey. This data is a strong indictment upon societal parent-child relationships. It further shows that parents spend more time with younger children and less and less with older ones. As a society, we are too busy.

Time spent with children, especially during their formative years, pays dividends in the long haul, as it helps children to develop a sense of purpose and confidence. While you may not be able to make every soccer practice, gymnastics routine, or piano rehearsal, you can certainly make enough of the child's events to show that you are interested in the things that are important to him or her. Frame or adjust your work schedule wherever possible to maximize the time spent with your kids. Taking kids to school in the morning is one way of getting the scoop on their day's events. Time in the car also gives parents time to reinforce family values, such as praying in the car with them, or better yet, teaching them to do so.

Picking kids up after school, with the attendant conversation, gives parents firsthand knowledge of how their day went. Such uninterrupted quality time provides you the opportunity to encourage them in many ways, such as, reinforcing confidence in their ability to pass the tests of schoolwork. It is also a great time to give them advice on how to handle the people or circumstances they will encounter. These conversations will allow you to keep a handle on your children's friends and activities through maintaining open lines of communication. Time spent with your children is never wasted unless you fail to realize its value.

Practical tips

1. Make time in your day that belongs to you and your child.

2. Show your interest in what interests your children by being at their activities whenever possible.

3. Create your own timeless moments with your child through fun activities.

Chapter Eight:

Don't Make Excuses for Your Child's Misbehavior

"I know my Johnny didn't do what they say he did. People are always blaming him for something." Such is the reasoning of the parent who suffers from the perils of excusitis. Unfortunately, too often I witness parents making excuses for the conduct—or should we say misconduct—of the child.

A youth was recently transferred to adult court with a major bond, following a series of criminal activities dating back over several years. He started out around age thirteen, with shoplifting, drug use, and burglary. The parents hired a private attorney to defend him and even paid for him to go into a drug rehab center for several months. Yet after getting out of the rehab center, he continued to pursue criminal conduct. He was later involved in several burglaries involving theft of firearms and their subsequent sale. The parents were still not convinced that their son had ever done anything wrong. After serving a lengthy juvenile commitment program for over a year, he got out and within a couple months was back with his guys and getting involved with more burglaries and auto thefts, including the burning of a vehicle that he had stolen. Once again, the parents were not convinced that their son had done anything wrong. The parents literally lost their business and their marriage because they refused to acknowledge the truth that their son was deeply involved in a one-man crime spree. Now he is in adult prison, his parents have divorced and also lost their business. Such is a horrible conclusion for parents who never took real control of their household and their children.

Letter from youth in Detention

Dear Honorable Judge Grimes

I am here today in court, because of the actions that I have done. I know from experience that the road I am on is not the one I want to go down. My childhood is not an excuse for my behavior. I know now that I am becoming a man and that brings a lot of responsibilities. I realize the bad things I have done in the past but I want to change my future because of these things. I sincerely want to become a better person, not only to myself but to the ones I love. I am here today to ask for one more chance to prove to you and my family that I can and will be a good and respectful citizen. I am sorry for all I have done and I promise to change my ways. Thank you for taking the time out to read this letter.

Sincerely,
T. K.

It is unfortunate that many parents do not connect the dots between their child's conduct at home and his or her potential to commit delinquent acts in the community. That is, until the child is apprehended by law enforcement and taken into custody. As the above letter describes, this youth knows that his conduct has been wrong. His parents on the other hand never made him own up to his conduct. It took the court system for him to make him own up to his delinquent behavior.

Most children know their parents better than the parents know their children. They know what they can get away with and what they cannot. Kids, even good kids, will push the envelope on occasion, and some will do so routinely. Parents must never make excuses for a child's misconduct. Some excuses that are commonly raised include:

- Not my child. My child would never do anything like that.

- My child doesn't have a dad at home.

- My child is ADD, ADHD, ODD or any of the host of alphabet labels, which while psychologically sound, still doesn't eliminate the fact that all of us, including our children, are given the opportunity to make choices along the path of our life. Rich or poor, male or female, black, white, Hispanic or otherwise we each get to choose our life's pathway on a daily basis. The daily choices are often small and indistinguishable, but often point us in the direction of success or failure.

- We don't have much money to buy Johnny what he needs. Yet the question must be asked, since when are the character traits of honesty, integrity, and hard work purchased at the local retail store or online? They are not.

They are the results of daily reinforcement of the values and standards you expect your child to live up to.

> *Parents must always be on their "A" game in order to keep up with the ever-changing demands of raising children and the things even good kids will try to get away with.*

- Five-year-old Lil Johnny's stealing of a cookie from the cookie jar when your back is turned and lying about it without consequences turns into shoplifting at twelve and stealing a car at fifteen, because he knows mom and dad will always bail him out and say it's not his fault. It's not his fault that the store manager put the candy bars near the checkout counter or that the woman left the keys in the car to run inside the store for a cold drink.

Even more incredulous are the excuses such as: "Everybody is against my child. The teacher gives him too much homework. The principal is always picking on Johnny. They are always telling him to quiet down in the hallway but not the other kids. The bus driver makes him move to another seat. The police officer always follows Johnny at school or at the mall shopping center. And don't forget, 'little Johnny' is on medication and sometimes forgets or refuses to take his meds. But it only happens when he misses two days of his medication for bipolar disorder. Johnny is really a good kid. He just has some problems. You know his daddy was an alcoholic and his auntie is a crack head." This parent, like so many others, makes excuses and wants others to understand "little Johnny's" temper tantrums. There is no excuse for a child to destroy the contents of a house including the television, computer, telephone, windows, and walls, under the guise of not getting what he wants.

But what does all of this have to do with the fact that everyone is given the opportunity to make it in this life? There are no free passes, and excuses for failure or misconduct do not bring positive rewards. Parents who minimize or excuse the misconduct of their children are setting those kids up for major problems down the road. The world is very unforgiving of excuses that justify misconduct or harm to others. The best way to stop the excusitis of little Johnny is to nip it in the bud. Only then will the child know that the parent loves him or her but will not excuse or support wrongdoing.

> *Most children know their parents better than the parents know their children; consequently, they know what they can get away with.*

> *He who loves his child but fails to discipline him is worst than an infidel. Proverbs 13:24(KJV)*

Those who experience a lack of being parented can engage in numerous forms of delinquent behavior. One of the often-missed parenting opportunities deals with setting limits. When parents fail to impose limits on children's behavior, the results are not pleasant. During my tenure on the bench, I have seen many parents stand in court and openly admit fear of their children. That fear did not develop overnight. Many of us have witnessed the out-of-control temper tantrums of three, four, and five-year-olds in the malls, or in retail or grocery stores. Too often instead of giving the child a strong tap on the rear end when the behavior occurs, many choose to ignore the behavior, laugh it off, get embarrassed, or bribe the child with a toy, candy, or ice-cream. My mother did not tolerate that conduct with me, my siblings or any other children that were around us growing up. You don't have to either.

Parents who fail to parent by refusing to impose limits on their little darlings create long-term consequences, and even cause their "little darlings" to grow up to become holy terrors. Such is the result of allowing behaviors that start out small to grow out of control.

Over the last few years, I have asked the students in my law classes at the Orlando-based Florida A&M College of Law, how many of them received physical spankings while growing up. The response was near unanimous. Next, I asked if they had friends who did not get disciplined by parents and what they were doing now. Their responses reflected that many of those friends who did not get corrected early in their lives ended up in trouble, did not finish high school, have struggled in life with multiple issues, and are certainly not as successful as this group of law students. Is there a connection between setting limits for children and physical discipline when necessary, with later success in life? Judging from this limited unscientific poll of approximately one hundred fifty students, there is a strong connection.

Keep in mind that I am not talking about abusing a child with outlandish, unnecessary beatings. I am saying that loving, physical discipline may be legally applied when necessary and appropriate, particularly during the formative years of a child's life. Using physical discipline to help establish limits for a child's conduct is necessary and permitted under the law. While I have had many parents tell me in open court that it is against the law to spank their child, the true reality is that spanking is permitted under the laws of my state. Specifically, *Florida Statutes* 39.01(2) and 984.03(2) provide that "corporal discipline of a child by a parent or legal custodian for disciplinary purposes does not in itself constitute abuse when it does not result in harm to the child."

If a parent waits until a child is a teenager to attempt to spank him it is too late, and such conduct opens a parent up to bigger problems. Abuse of a child is illegal, but spanking to correct a child is legal and permitted under our laws. Parents must understand the difference and not allow children to intimidate them with such statements such as, "You cannot spank me, because you will go to jail." A spanking is given to correct behavior and should be age appropriate and done out of love. Abuse, on the other hand, leaves severe markings, causes physical or emotional injury to a child, and can cause long-term negative effects. While some will say the difference between abuse and discipline is a gray area, in reality, a loving parent truly understands the distinction. I personally know of no one from my generation who grew up in small-town America who did not receive spankings, especially in the formative years of their youth. These same people, who were disciplined by loving parents, were taught to have respect for self and others. Many of these individuals successfully occupy leadership positions in business, government, education, entertainment, and every other category of our society. Our parents must have done something right, considering the results.

Practical Tips

1. Never make excuses for your child's misconduct. Once you start doing so, the child will continue to engage in an ever increasing pattern of misbehavior.

2. Parents should never allow children to play one parent against the other.

3. Psychological labels, such as ADD, ADHD, ODD, etc., must never become an excuse for not holding children responsible for the choices they make.

4. Corrective discipline, including spankings when necessary, is not prohibited by law.

Chapter Nine:

Don't Overprotect Your Kids

> *Keeping kids too close to the nest will slow their development and limit their potential for success.*

The opposite of allowing kids to run wild without discipline or control is to be overprotective or overcontrol them. Overprotective parents may have experienced difficulty in having children or lost a child by tragic accident or unexpected illness. They may attempt to make up for their fear or unfortunate occurrence by being overprotective of the miracle child who was born out of difficulty or the one who survived the tragedy that caused the loss of a sibling.

While it is common and expected for parents to be doting over their kids when they are young, they should use wisdom in slowly releasing the reigns as a child grows and matures. When the parent attempts to dominate or overcontrol the child's life, maturing children will tend to either be deceitful toward the parents or outright rebellious.

Deceitfulness leads to kids putting on a "Doctor Jekyll and Mr. Hyde" personality. In their parent's presence, they are darling angels. Outside their presence, the child takes on a different persona—one who will try anything, be it illicit sex, drugs, gang-banging, or other anti-social behavior. All the while, he or she presents an image to the parents that everything is well. A youth comes to mind who appeared before me several times from ages twelve to seventeen. His mother was a professional in the criminal justice system and never seemed to believe that her son was out of control. It was always the school officials or law enforcement who treated her son unfairly. Yet this same youth was confirmed by law enforcement as the leader in a local gang chapter. He proudly displayed gang symbols as he posed for photographs with other gang members on the school campus, but yet his mother still remained in denial, despite being shown copies of the photographs. Less than a month after completing a year-long juvenile commitment program, he was arrested after crashing the getaway car following the commission of a home invasion with a firearm. At seventeen years old, he was recently sentenced to eighteen years in state prison following the transfer of his case to adult court.

Parents whose children play the game of deceit are the ones who are most shocked by their child being arrested for delinquent behavior. They often say, "I did everything that I could. He was under my control all the time." But control or perceived control, absent the teachings of trust, discipline, and values, will not make the child do right. Parents must strike a balance between overcontrol and lack of control as they teach core values. Overcontrolled youth may be drawn to other controlling people in their lives who make decisions for them. They become followers and are ripe targets for gang association. Both girls and guys develop into "man-pleasers," seeking to please those who lead them around or make decisions for them, just like Momma did. They become followers who are led around by the "flavor of the week" being offered by gang leaders, abusers, users, or controllers because they were never taught to think for themselves. Momma was their cover and whenever they got away from Momma, they sought out another cover, even if it was the wrong one.

These youth are ill-equipped to face the world's challenges and may find themselves following the lead of a stronger personality who controls them like their Momma did. They get out from under their parent's authority by running away and end up the same way—rebelling, only to end up in a worse situation. They rebel in an effort to find themselves. Unfortunately, finding themselves usually means they look for love and acceptance in all the wrong places. In all likelihood, those places are not the ones the parents expected. These parents never saw the problem coming.

Letter from Young Man in Detention Center to Judge

Dear Judge Grimes,

I've been in the Detention Center for twenty-three days as of today. My visit here has given me time to clear my mind and gather my thoughts of what I need to do to succeed and better my ways of thinking. It's also made me realize that my grandparents don't do much good for me, even though they gave me a lot of money to get away from my mother. I think as I said before in the first letter that moving out of state with my grandparents should not be allowed. Also, on my personal interest I've decided on my own that I should have little or no contact with them. [Author's note: Grandparents paid for grandson's hotel rooms and supplied money to him while youth was on runaway status from local home and probation supervision for over a month, including trips to Key West and North Carolina.] Whether or not you decide it's for the right cause to send me, I would still like to obtain my GED and start college. I plan to go to Daytona State for a degree in Marine Engineering and I could start that in the fall or after a program. I honestly believe that if you just give me one last chance, I not only think but I know that I can turn it around for the better and straighten my life out by doing everything required on my probation and get my education finished now before it's too late. Also I will continue with the ADOP (Adolescent Drug Outpatient Program) and pass all my tests. Drugs get you nowhere in life except trouble and I'm done being in trouble. For once I want to stay out of trouble and actually be able to go out and be trusted. I'm ready to step up to my actions and responsibility, if you will give me one last chance. I swear you won't ever see me in front of you again.

Sincerely,

D. S.

Practical Tips

1. Maintain a balance between freedom and control of the child. Too much of either can be detrimental.

2. Explain to children as they mature into adolescence and teen years that trust and responsibility go hand in hand. Breaching either results in loss of privileges and freedom.

3. While parents must always consider a child's safety, overcontrol will limit the ability of the child to properly mature into adulthood.

Chapter Ten:

Keep a Close Eye on the Friends They Keep

> *The friends that a child hangs out with will influence the success or failure of that child.*

There is an old maxim, "Birds of a feather flock together." People in general and children in particular, hang out with similar-type individuals. I have often told young people the adage, "if you show me your five closest friends, I will show you your future."

Each human being, adult or child, becomes the product of his or her influences. But where do these influences come from? They are primarily from the environment in which we each live and operate on a daily basis. When children are young, they absorb their environment whether it is good or bad. When love is given by a parent, children respond with love. On the other hand, undue criticism often results in an attitude of insecurity, which in turn opens the door for other problems, including gravitating to the false promises of those whose true motives are to use them for their own purposes.

When kids enter school, an entirely new environment is opened up to them. As they progress in school, the influence of home gives way to the interaction of friends. Suddenly, new ways of thinking emerge. They are exposed to new ideas, not just from the classroom, but in the hallways, on the playground, and even on the school bus. The priorities in their lives refocus from pleasing parents to pleasing friends. And here is the rub. Do you know who your child's friends are? Parents, this is a critical time for communication between you and your child.

Who are they hanging out with at school? In school, musicians hang out with other musicians. Athletes bond with other athletes. Artists associate with artists. Gang members hang out with their gang members. Who are they talking to on the telephones, text messaging on the cell phone, or posting and e-mailing on MySpace or Facebook? Have you checked their computer or looked at their "friends" list? What photos have they posted of themselves on the web? Are they posting provocative sexual images online or sending nude images of themselves to others? Are they showing gang photos holding an AK-47 machine gun as they are smoking a blunt (marijuana) or showcasing the latest concoction of drug paraphernalia or stolen money? Photos with these images have come to my attention and review.

In the last few years, I have witnessed an increase in documented group criminal activity among the youth appearing before me. While such gang activity is certainly not limited by blood ties, two families come immediately to mind as examples of family-style gang conduct.

In one family, two brothers became leaders of their own gang, adopting the label of "The Bloods" as their gang of choice.

They drew other youth into the fold by influence, threats, and intimidation. They engaged in car and home burglaries and fights, and they used weapons wherever they felt they were needed. Both brothers ended up serving lengthy juvenile commitment programs along with two of their cousins and other associates. Yet in spite of multiple times in court and mounds of evidence, their mother always seemed in denial—clueless of what was happening under her nose with her sons and the people who hung out at her house. Each of these sons has recently been resentenced to lengthy juvenile commitment programs.

In a different example, three teenage sisters and their baby brother moved to Florida from New York to live with their grandmother. Both mom and dad were out of the picture due to drugs and prison. These three sisters associated with a Hispanic gang and became terrors in their neighborhood. They fought other kids. They shoplifted from stores and burglarized cars and houses. They went to school when they chose and usually were suspended for threatening teachers, administrators, or other students. The grandmother was not deceived nor did she make excuses for their conduct, as each of the three girls ended up in custody, sometimes even at the same time. Finally, one of the sisters broke out of the pack and decided to get on the right track. At last contact, she had completed her GED and enrolled in school to become a nurse. Slowly but surely, her changes seem to be influencing the other two sisters, each of whom has spent time in commitment programs. The youngest brother attempted to start down a similar road of criminality, but abruptly changed his attitude when an uncle moved into the home to assist the grandmother by taking charge of an out-of-control situation. As far as the other two girls are concerned, they have reportedly changed their ways after being released from custody and are now pursuing a normal teen life.

An all-too-often answer to the question, "How did you get yourself in this mess?" is "I was just hanging out with my friends." Unfortunately, these were not the friends who were going to class, getting their school work done, and staying out of trouble. These were the ones who were cutting class to have a "Jack Daniel's" or weed (marijuana) party. They walk in the front door of the school, bypass class, and leave through the rear exit. Then they sneak off campus to link up with others and proceed to party over at the house of Joe's mamma's boyfriend's next door neighbor who is out of town for a month.

These friends often dare one another to partake in criminal activities such as breaking into the house down the street because "those people are gone up north on vacation." In one such instance, a group of kids left school to party, and while at their friend's house, they found a spare set of house keys belonging to a neighbor who was out of town on vacation. They went to the neighbor's house, let themselves in, and managed to find the spare set of keys to the car sitting in the garage. They decided to take the car out for a day of joyriding. After picking up a few of their friends, they all hung out for the day until it was time to get back to school before the buses left. As the inexperienced fifteen-year-old driver sped back to the school, she took a curve too fast, lost control of the car, and the overcrowded vehicle overturned. A fourteen-year-old female was ejected from the vehicle, which rolled over her, and she subsequently died from her injuries at the hospital. The driver, the other occupants, and each of the family members' lives are forever changed as a result of what was perceived by some as a day of fun. Friends who should have been in school, ended up causing hurt and pain to several families, including the homeowners, the car owners, the driver, and the deceased, whose life was cut short too early. A giant hole was left in the hearts of parents who lost a child, and a "child-driver" faces the life-changing consequences of careless driving resulting in the negligent death of a friend. That incident will follow her for the rest of her life.

"Friends" always seem to be the influence that causes some to smoke weed and others to drink a few beers. In one instance, friends were at a house drinking and smoking weed, when a teenager found his dad's gun. While horsing around, he accidentally discharged a gun into the brain of his nine-year-old brother who happened to walk into his brother's room at the wrong time, killing him instantly. "Friends" have raided liquor cabinets of parents and got drunk while mixing light and dark liquors together. They hold "rainbow parties" where everyone raids their parent's medicine cabinet and brings whatever prescription drugs they can find to the party. There, the pills are placed in a bowl or passed out indiscriminately, without regard to the dangers presented by taking a substance for which they don't have a clue as to its effects.

In one situation, after sharing their parents' medications as part of a rainbow party with another friend, two girls awoke to find themselves disrobed and sexed by several of their so-called friends and the friend's cousins. One girl later discovered that she was pregnant, and both of the girls were positive for sexually transmitted diseases. These negative friends will help others to do all of the above in the name of friendship and even hide them out at the house of a friendly parent. This is usually the place where rules are nonexistent and kids come and go as they please. All the while, the house parents condone the conduct because the kids use the excuse that the other child's mom put her out and she has nowhere to go.

Friends like these never seem to show up in court to check on the one who was arrested. These purported friends never volunteer to do the time for the one who broke the law and is in custody. These friends help kids to slip in or out of houses, through bedroom windows after parents are asleep, so they can go to the party of the week or have sex with their boyfriend in the parent's house. In one reported case, a father awakened to let the dog out at 4:00 AM, and upon hearing noises coming from his daughter's room, opened the door to see a naked male standing over his daughter's bed. He picked up a baseball bat and beat the naked man out of his house, only to later find out that this was his fifteen-year-old daughter's boyfriend who had been slipping into her bedroom window for the last several months. The crowning irony was that the responding rookie police officer arrested the father for battery on the intruder. Fortunately, reason and common sense prevailed as the charges were quickly dropped by the State Attorney's office. Under *Florida Statutes* 776.012, and in an increasing number of other jurisdictions, "homeowners may use lethal force to protect themselves and the occupants of their home or vehicle if they feel threatened." In this instance, the father was justified, as he thought that he was protecting his daughter from the perceived intruder.

And, of course, what about youth who begin to run with their negative friends and end up proclaiming them as "family"? It starts out with being told that these new friends care more about the teen than the teen's own parents. These same friends introduce them to other family members. And, if they truly want to be loved and cared for, all they have to do is go the next step and swear their allegiance to the family. By any other definition, this family is known as a gang.

Gangs initiate their members in different ways, but often youth are physically beaten into the gang family or in the case of a female, are "sexed" into the family. This usually requires the girl to have sex with the gang leader or his designees, one after another, in a ritualistic ceremony. Many times gangs require their new initiates to prove their loyalty to the family by robbing, stealing, burglarizing, or "backing down" someone the gang doesn't like. Often the victim is an innocent person. Another approach is to trample on another gang's territory in defiance of their so called authority, by tagging or painting their symbol on a rival gang's wall, fence, or building. Many times these gangs use teen gathering places such as a park, basketball courts, or even school events to isolate and recruit new members. Many states have passed legislation to prohibit such conduct but it remains difficult to enforce.

Parents should monitor the clothing and accessories worn by their children, especially following the transition from adolescence to teens. When kids start wearing attire resembling uniforms that have not been required by their school, it is time to find out what is going on with your child. While matching black or khaki clothing is currently popular as an urban trend, many teens are using the attire as gang-uniforms. Sometimes, kids will adopt sports paraphernalia such as jerseys or baseball caps of a certain color to represent their gang's identity. Blue, red, black and gold are among prominent colors for some of the nationally known gangs. Large chains with symbols such as area codes, symbolic guns, brass knuckles, or other weapons are identifiers. Sneakers with special artwork, belt buckles, and folded bandanas are also used to identify gang members to one another.

In my local county, which has a population of less than 500,000 persons, the sheriff's agency has published reports tracking nearly one hundred gangs and over one thousand members or affiliates. These include well-known violent motorcycle gangs as well as local teen hustlers who focus on property crimes to make a quick buck to support their habits while savoring the thrill of the moment.

It is not unheard of for multiple members of the same family to get involved in gang or gang-like activity. Neither is such conduct limited to the male gender alone. The ethnicities of these gang members run the gamut from Caucasian, African-American, Hispanic, and Asian. Their families seem to embrace drama or at a minimum fail to monitor the activities of the youth.

One mother always made excuses for the conduct of each of her sons. They were two years apart and considered themselves to be part of the Bloods gang. They burglarized cars and houses, sold and smoked marijuana, got in serious fights with others, and both ended up in commitment programs—what some might call juvenile prisons—each serving a twelve- to twenty-four-month period of confinement. One of the guys decided to hook up with a female from a rival gang that called themselves Tri-State. The two of them had a private party that left each of them drunk, disheveled, and unconscious. The sister of the female found her unclothed in an abandoned house where she and the rival gang member were both passed out on the floor with empty liquor bottles and beer cans strewn around. While in the world of gangs, such conduct is usually considered an act of war, here were two teens who knew each other from the neighborhood and each along with their family members always seemed to be pushing the envelope. The male represented the Bloods and the female represented Tri-State in some sort of sex-out, an equivalent to the Wild West days of a shoot-out at the O.K. Corral. In both families, parental control was severely lacking.

In another family, a set of twin brothers followed the same path of delinquency that their older sister had embarked upon. They were constantly fighting other persons, even adults, and on multiple occasions, one or the other would beat up their mother. During their last encounter in court, following an attack on their stepfather who they thought was beating their mother, their grandmother stated that their mother had never set any limits on the boys from the time they were eight years old. She had told them at that time to do whatever they wanted, as long as they did not bother her. In essence, these kids raised themselves with very little parental supervision or accountability, except that which was imposed upon them by the court when they were arrested for their misconduct. Both youth, now eighteen, have graduated to adult court with pending felony charges.

Another such family has seen each of the three kids end up in front of me. The oldest son set the pattern followed by his sister and then the younger brother. Each developed a drug habit of marijuana, cocaine, and pills. Their household was always in turmoil. The youth seemed to take turns fighting, stealing, and threatening anyone who got in their way. The mother started the entire cycle with her own conduct and condoned the kid's behavior by letting them do as they pleased. The older son is now facing adult drug charges. The sister, now a young adult, has lost custody of her two children following two failed residential drug treatment programs and is now serving a stint in the county jail. The mother continues to deny that she is the real problem in the family, in spite of the fact that a cyclone of drama always seems to be swirling around her.

On one occasion, one of my court staff overheard another problem mother cursing her daughter out in the hallway of the courthouse for refusing to share her drugs with the mother. As if that was not incredible, another mother appeared in court to request the release of her daughter from custody. When I confronted that mother about her fifteen-year-old daughter, who was on probation, being found in bed with a known drug dealer in the mother's home during the execution of a search warrant, she replied that it was her daughter's bedroom and the daughter could do as she pleased. Is it any wonder that these youth are delinquent, when the parents are acting more like their friends than the responsible adults that they are supposed to be?

True friends want what is best for another and will look out for and encourage one another to achieve greatness. On the other extreme, negative friends will bring a youth down into the gutter. The true friend will stick closer than a brother. The false friend will usually break camp and run when they are caught in their mischief, leaving the other friend to make it on his own. Which would you choose as friends for your son or daughter? Keep a close check on your child's friends. Invite them over to your house so you can get to know them instead of allowing your kids to spend the night at the friend's house whose parents you do not know. The strategy of going over to a friend's house to visit or spend the night has opened the door for many unsupervised periods of time, leading to unexpected mischief with long-term consequences. According to U.S. Department of Juvenile Justice delinquency statistics published in 2006, "the time from the end of the school day until 7:00 PM is the most vulnerable period for delinquent misconduct, particularly violent offenses, as most parents are still at work and the kids are unsupervised."

Help your children to make wise choices in the selection of their friends. Don't choose their friends for them, but put them in environments where the type of kids who hang out there will be the caliber for which there is a greater likelihood of positive, not negative, influences. Many of the presentencing reports that I have reviewed over the years indicate that the delinquent youth in front of me, "does not attend church, and is not involved in any structured community activity." My grandmother often said, "An idle mind is a playground for the devil." Keep children busy and supervised. Far too many of our youth have too much nonproductive, unsupervised time on their hands, and the result is an increase in delinquent behavior.

Encourage children to participate in structured activities that build their self-esteem, especially while they are young. The younger kids are when they get started in such activities, the better. Positively structured activities that also build friendships include getting involved in a solid teaching church and its youth group activities, the YMCA, the Boys or Girls Club, municipal recreation leagues, individual and team sports, or other organized and supervised youth programs. Frequent trips to the library with parents and friends while children are young will develop an appreciation for reading. Creating youth book clubs, which meet at your home or that of another trusted parent, is a great self-esteem and camaraderie builder. Boy Scouts, Girl Scouts, Boy's or Girl's Clubs, youth athletic programs, school or community-sponsored organizations, and other youth-oriented organizations are also wonderful methods of building self-esteem. In addition, these activities develop positive habits of unselfishness, team building, interdependence and independence, while teaching useful skills that will be helpful later in life. Leadership skills such as conducting a meeting while using parliamentary procedure, learning to debate, and/or public speaking can be developed in these positively structured activities.

While these suggestions are not the absolute answers for every situation, they represent ideas and suggestions that will give direction to a parent seeking to steer the child toward positive friends and influences. Absent positive parental involvement in children's lives, kids are left to their own choices—which may or may not be good ones. Parents should not look at their children in the present moment alone. They should also keep them involved in positive activities that will develop their talents, with an eye toward going to college or otherwise pursuing their dreams. How soon should this start? The sooner the change starts, the better. Kids begin to develop interpersonal skills at a very early age. However, keep in mind that children's group activities should always be age appropriate. Even as teens reach the ages when they begin to feel that they know it all, maintaining an eye on their associates is critical to their success. Have them invite their friends over to the house—such as for a meal, a cookout, or another weekend activity. That will give you a chance to meet their friends and to begin a subtle realignment of their friends or associates if needed or certainly at a minimum to give you some contact information that may be helpful in the future. Although realigning children away from negative friends may be a little more difficult, it is still worth the effort.

I have often conditioned probation requirements to include that youth must engage in positive community activities, such as some of those listed herein. The goal, as you guessed it, is to realign their friends and contacts from negative peers to positive ones. Change the friends they run with and their actions will follow. The earlier these new relationships are created, the better.

These relationships among children also build strength and cohesiveness in the family and community. Parents begin talking and socializing with other positive parents. This leads to parental participation in school activities and interaction with teachers and school administrators. All of this revolves around the children who will see the active role of the parents in their education and upgrade the child's respect for the time spent and sacrifices made by their parents. This also will enhance the parent-teacher-student relationship.

Practical Tips

1. Know the names of your children's closest friends and their parents, including contact information.

2. Encourage your children through positive interactions and activities with other young people who exhibit good conduct.

3. Keep an eye on the clothing your kids are wearing. If there is a sudden change in their attire, monitor to see if others are wearing similar gang paraphernalia. These items include but are not limited to certain colors worn, bandanas, markings, tattoos, etc. Check out internet web sites that show examples of gang paraphernalia including shirts, jeans, sneakers, and bandanas. If your son or daughter appears to be wearing a self-imposed uniform, it warrants further inquiry.

4. Create an environment for kids to associate with other like-minded youth, particularly when they are young.

5. Keep children busy through supervised activities, such as sports, music, clubs, scouting, etc.

6. Invite their friends to your house for a cookout or other activities as a way of monitoring their conduct and choice of associates.

7. Get involved with the things that your child likes, not as a friend but as a supportive parent. This will also give you a chance to keep up with his or her activities.

Chapter Eleven:

Set and Keep Rules for the House

He who pays the rent makes the rules.

W*ebster's New College Dictionary* defines "rules" as "an authoritative direction for conduct, a usual or customary course of action, or to keep within proper limits." Rules are a set of standards by which a group of like-minded individuals, brought together by common purpose, location, or goals, agree to abide. Rules may be the result of agreement or imposition. In sports, rules provide a standard of conduct through which athletes are judged based on a level playing field. Spectator sports such as football, basketball, baseball, golf, and swimming have rules that are created by a sanctioning body such as the National Collegiate Athletic Association, the National Football League, National Basketball Association, Major League Baseball Association, etc. Even the Olympic Games have rules that must be followed in order for record-breaking performances to mean anything when compared with similar events from yesteryear.

In society, rules or laws are adopted by governing bodies such as legislatures or municipal governments and enforced for the peaceful good of the citizenry. This is also true in schools, churches, clubs, or anywhere that a group of individuals gather together. Rules are needed in order to further a peaceful coexistence among students and teachers, parishioners and pastors, or club leadership and members. If rules are needed in those settings, does it not follow that rules are necessary in the most fundamental unit of society, the family home?

Dating back to the Garden of Eden, the family unit is the oldest institution on planet Earth. With the creation of Adam and Eve, rules were established for the peaceful coexistence of the Supreme Being and his creation. But for the breaking of the rules as spelled out in Genesis 2:17, "not to eat the fruit of the tree of knowledge of good and evil, in the center of the garden," mankind and his relationships would be far different today. Somehow, mankind followed the rule of Genesis 1:28 to be "fruitful and multiply," but we violated the one that ultimately opened the door for death and disorder to enter.

In the same manner, it is extremely important that parents establish and enforce rules of the house. While it is the nature of human beings, especially children, to test the limits, "house rules" are needed to create an environment where parents and children can peacefully coexist.

I find it interesting that many youth who come before me are shocked when I impose certain rules of conduct that they must follow during the time their case is pending before the court. In particular, I have seen puzzled looks when I tell them they must live at home with parents or custodians; follow a set curfew, usually 7:00 PM; obey the rules of the house and not disrupt or cause harm to anyone in the household; avoid contact with negative individuals; not consume any alcohol, cigarettes, or illegal drugs; and go to school daily without unexcused absences, tardies, or behavior problems. Many of these youth look at me as if I was speaking a foreign language. Some glare back in defiance while others have the shocked look of a deer blinded by headlights. Either they have never had any house rules imposed upon them by their parents or, even worse, they have figured out that the parents can't tell them what to do. In either scenario, this represents a recipe for chaos, which is part of why they are in court.

Why are rules important? Not only do they help to create a peaceful coexistence for all concerned, rules also help in the following ways:

1. Create respect for authority

2. Set minimum standards for acceptable conduct

3. Create a zone of safety and protection for children

4. Establish expectations of behavior and performance at home, in school, and among siblings

5. Create a level of discipline and respect which will follow children into their adult life and beyond

6. Remind children that parents love them and are willing to establish limits that will protect them from harm

House rules will vary according to the age of the children. What is appropriate for infants and prekindergarten children is not the same for adolescents and teens. Listed below are some sample suggestions that may be helpful to consider as you develop your own house rules.

Rules for Infants and Young Children

Establish a routine sleep schedule. While an infant's eating and sleeping are primarily dictated by need in the first few months, the sooner the child is placed on a regular sleeping pattern, the sooner the child will adapt to the routine. Sleep is critical to the growth and development of children. Regular sleep helps eliminate crankiness and many behavioral problems. Once a good sleep pattern is established, routines for eating, playing, and other activities can be built in.

Never allow television to dictate the child's sleep pattern. Many of the adolescents and teens who appear before me in delinquency court have sleeping problems, often staying up all night watching television or playing video games. As a result, they routinely oversleep and are late or absent from school. They commonly experience truancy and behavior problems. Parents often say, "The child won't get up in the morning, even though I wake him up." Yet, these same youth were never required to have a disciplined sleep schedule dating back to the early years of infancy. The parent must control the house, the television, and their child's sleep schedule in order to get them on the right track.

Rules for School Age Children and Adolescents

As children begin to attend school they experience broader social exposure. While the home and family have largely shaped their outlook on life up until this point, they now begin to regularly interact with others of their same age group. An unseen tug-of-war begins between the family and their friends. Parents with a long-term vision must establish a strong familial foundation at this time that will be able to hold up against the forces to which the children will be exposed. I suggest the use of a framework that includes clear expectations that the child will regularly attend school, respect all adults including teachers and school staff, stay focused in class and complete each assignment, ask for help from the teacher when needed, and wear neat, age-appropriate clothing that will not create distractions in school. When school is out, children's time must be monitored for their safety and well-being. Whether parents pick them up from school, they catch the bus, or walk home, there must be a safety plan established that makes sure they arrive home safe and sound each day. Where there is a one parent family, reach out to other trusted adults for help in making sure the children arrive home safe and sound.

Once the children are at home, they should complete their homework first before anything else. Limit television during the school week, if at all. The same goes for video games or use of the internet for social or entertainment purposes. I strongly suggest a consistent bedtime for children which will allow them to have a full night's sleep. For some children, a full night's sleep is ten hours. As children age, a full night's sleep is eight hours. Parents will be able to determine the sleep needs of their children by watching how kids react in the morning. If they are cranky when they awaken, then an earlier bedtime may be needed, so that they consistently awaken at the same time each morning with clarity and energy for the day ahead.

Why a Curfew?

The primary purpose of curfew is safety for the child. During school nights, my parents believed I should be home before dark unless I had supervised school activities. The later the child is out of the home, away from adult supervision, the greater the risk of accidents or delinquent conduct. Weekend curfews are a privilege, and while parents may give older kids more freedom for activities such as movies, sporting events, or shopping, the reasonableness of the curfew should be tempered with the positive conduct of the youth. While a fourteen-year-old could be allowed to attend a structured activity as long as there is adult supervision, the parents, not the child, should dictate the time of the curfew. Keep in mind, that thirteen and seventeen-year-olds mixing together unsupervised can be a source of potential problems. Many thirteen and fourteen-year-old girls are often fascinated by the attention received from males that are sixteen to eighteen years old and even older. In the absence of adult supervision, these scenarios are problems waiting to happen. Parents should not be duped into thinking this situation only occurs with someone else's child, not their own. Without proper supervision, many problems can occur that would otherwise have never existed.

A few months back, an eleven-year-old girl appeared in front of me on shoplifting charges. By appearance alone, she looked much older than her age, with well-coiffed hair and nails, fashionable clothing, jewelry, and the like. When discussing whether the child could be trusted to abide by a 7:00 PM curfew and my standard judicial behavior order, the grandmother replied, "She doesn't listen or follow any rules. She stays out late with her sixteen-year-old boyfriend." Upon further inquiry as to the identity of the sixteen-year-old boyfriend, I recognized his name as a youth who had appeared before me multiple times and had recently been transferred by me to adult court on charges of armed robbery with a firearm, carjacking, grand theft auto, and a host of other felony charges. Prior to the new charges, he had just completed a nine-month commitment program for domestic violence on a fifteen-year-old girlfriend. Of course, the eleven-year-old did not know anything about the fifteen-year-old girlfriend. Had the eleven-year-old been supervised and curfew-restricted, the likelihood of her developing a relationship with "Mr. Bad Boy" would have been further minimized. I ended up having to take the young lady into custody based on the disrespect she exhibited in court toward her grandmother and her open defiance of the court's authority. Ironically, a routine medical screening while she was in custody disclosed that she was pregnant by, guess who, the same young man mentioned earlier. She has since given birth, but recently appeared back in front of me for violating probation. She missed school repeatedly and hangs out with other delinquents. Not only is her absent father in prison, but so is the young man who impregnated her. He is serving a seven-year adult sentence, which he must do, day for day. Now, at the ripe old age of thirteen, she doesn't like school or supervision. Respect for her mother or grandmother is marginal at best. Because of the teen's attitude, conduct, and lax adult supervision, it is just a matter of time before the scenario is repeated and additional children are born. As with this teen mother, whose birth mother was also a teenager, the new babies are at a higher risk of being taken into foster care because the teen mother has very little time for children. She is too busy "getting her groove on." Prior to her appearance in court, this thirteen-year-old girl put herself at risk as she and the baby were passengers in a car driven by her nineteen-year-old cousin who sought to avoid a traffic stop and turned it into a high-speed chase. While they successfully eluded the police officers and abandoned the vehicle with the baby seat still in the back seat of the car, the baby was put at risk. Both the driver and the passenger were quickly found, and the driver was arrested.

Many parents are unaware that a significant number of today's teenage girls are attracted to "bad boy" images. Much of this attraction stems from video images amplified by the media. While a curfew alone will not fully protect the girls from getting caught up with these bad boys, when coupled with adult supervision, it will certainly be easier to monitor the type of friends with whom these girls hang out.

While one might think that school attendance should be a "no-brainer," there are too many youth who choose not to attend school, and parents are not holding them accountable. How does a child drop out of school in the sixth, seventh or eighth grade without a parent's knowledge or consent? Yet, it is happening based on flimsy excuses such as, "My teachers don't like me." Others attend school, but selectively cut classes, while others disrupt classes with their misconduct. Each school district has programs designed to help children with special needs, particularly to help reduce truancy and promote educational development. Parents should establish and maintain contact with their child's teachers and school officials from the very first day of kindergarten and continue until that child graduates from high school. Does it take extra effort? Yes, it does. This is why parents need to be willing to sacrifice for the long-term betterment of their children.

Set nonnegotiable family time. Spending dinner hour together is a great way of keeping up with your child's daily activities. Create other such family activities that will foster communication. Again, the earlier you start with this approach, the more accepting the children will be to the tradition. While some teens may be rebellious to the notion of spending quality family time together, the sooner you introduce this idea the better.

> *Children respond best when there are clear rules and limits set for their conduct.*

There are many other rules that can be adopted to benefit kids, such as no eating in the family room, no eating while watching television, making beds and cleaning bedrooms daily before doing anything else, hanging up clothes, putting dirty clothes in a hamper and not on the floor, not eating in the bedroom, putting shoes in the closet and not wherever you take them off; washing the dishes and taking out the garbage without being told, etc. Parents need to establish reasonable rules of conduct for their children. When you fail to do so at home, it is not long before the undisciplined conduct raises its ugly head elsewhere.

I am a firm believer that "he, who pays the rent, makes the rules." Too many youth have stood in front of me dressed in the latest fashion jeans, sneakers, tops, jewelry, and hairdos, without a clue as to the time and effort that it took for their parents to pay for those things. That alone is astounding, but even more so is when they stand there in total disrespect of the one who paid for those items. Of course, the blame doesn't belong to the kids alone. The parents ceded control to the kids long before they stood in court, in spite of their attempts to buy the kids off with sneakers and jewelry. They seem to believe that material expressions of love would bring about a similar response from the kids. But it did not. Instead they often find themselves feeding a bottomless pit of parental guilt, childhood selfishness, and increasing attitudes of ungratefulness that money will never fill. Parents, the time to take back your power and authority is overdue. Further delays will only result in problems that are increasingly difficult. I personally feel that it is a sign of abuse and neglect for a parent to surrender their house and rules to a child who "does not know what he does not know." It is as dangerous to let a child run the house as it would be to give car keys and a car to an eight-year-old. They may have a lot of zeal, but knowledge and ability are sorely lacking.

Parents, it is not only okay to make rules for your house, you are expected to by God and man. As stated earlier, children respond best when parents set limits for their behavior and conduct. The sooner those limits are put in place, the better.

Practical Tips

1. Parents should set rules of the house that are reasonable, enforceable, and flexible depending on the age of the children.

2. Children should not disrespect, disrupt, or cause harm to anyone in the house.

3. A curfew is not a punishment, but a safety device.

4. Standard bedtimes and wake-up times help ensure consistency in conduct and school performance.

5. Clothing should be neat and age appropriate, without creating distractions for others.

Chapter Twelve:

Don't Overlove a Child to Replace the Absence of a Spouse

> *Kids are smart enough to seize the moment and control a parent if the parent is not alert, especially during times of grief and emotional pain.*

All parents love their children. But many love their children in ways that cripple rather than empower them. One such example of this wrong way of loving a child was exhibited recently in open court by the following dialogue.

"Your honor, my son is fourteen years old. He is not a bad kid. He didn't start getting in trouble until we moved into the neighborhood, and he started hanging out with those bad kids. Please let him out of detention."

"But ma'am, your son is charged in six different car and house burglaries with different codefendants in four of the cases. There were also two burglaries that he is alleged to have committed by himself. Looking at the police reports, these charges did not all occur last night, but are spread out over the last two months, even while he was out of custody awaiting trial on the first two."

"But your honor, you don't understand, I am a single mom and it is just the two of us. His dad left when he was a baby, and without my son, I don't know what I am going to do. Could you please let him come home?"

This scenario occurs much too often. Many mothers make excuses for their son's misconduct because they have elevated the son's status to that of being the man of the house. While the idea of the son as the male figure who carries out responsibilities for chores following the parent's divorce or in lieu of an otherwise absent father is laudable, when the relationship becomes unbalanced, disaster can occur. Allowing the young male to have free rein of the house so much that by the time he is fifteen or sixteen he is dictating to the mother what he will or will not do, is unacceptable.

In one such case, a young man was brought back into custody after being released on house arrest for burglary charges. He had become so angry at his mother for not allowing him to leave home after the 7:00 PM. court-imposed curfew that he began to destroy the house, including the television, desktop computer, the coffee table, bedroom windows, vases, wall hangings, pictures, etc. Yet, mom who initially called 911, refused to press charges. Even though his actions violated the conditions of his court-ordered release, she still made excuses for his conduct by claiming the property all belonged to her son and he should not be charged with destroying his own property.

Now when or how did a sixteen- or seventeen-year-old furnish a home for which his parents are paying the rent or mortgage? Once again, a mother is making excuses for the son's misconduct.

But the added twist is that this mother has substituted the love for this "man-child" as a replacement for the lost love of a spouse. Now this is not intended to suggest a kinky relationship. It is instead an emotional attachment or soul tie that started when the mother became a single mom and began to focus only on Lil Johnny. Lil Johnny's conduct, no matter how rotten, became cute. Lil Johnny's tantrums in the department store were not rewarded with consequences, but ice cream. Lil Johnny's poor grades or misconduct became acceptable because mom works two jobs and is too tired to help him with homework, or has some other excuse.

"Lil Johnny acted out in school because he didn't take his medicine." "The pills are too big, and I forgot to leave them on the kitchen counter as I rushed out to work." "He didn't get up for school because he stayed up late watching television and playing video games." Because, because, because …

The Lil Johnnies have learned how to manipulate their mothers. Often, as these young boys grow up, limits have not been set for them and they believe they can do whatever they desire. Mom is viewed as an equal and not as an authority figure. She condones the conduct and treats Lil Johnny as her "little man." As Johnny grows up, he begins to perceive himself as the man of the house, which he has been unwittingly called by Mom many times. In extreme cases, he begins to take on attributes of dictating to his mother what she can and cannot do. Unless mom checks this conduct early on, Lil Johnny goes on to become a terror who tells mom what he will or will not do, causing the parent-child roles to be reversed. As this "man-child" grows in physical stature, often bigger than mom, he also becomes more demanding and aggressive in order to get what he wants. Cussing, pushing, and shoving mom around means nothing to him. Watching her cry has no effect. He has learned over the years that he will get whatever he sets his mind on. If it takes a tantrum in a store at age five in order to get a toy, or a screaming match with Mom at sixteen to get the keys to the car, he knows he will win because he has done so before. Mom, in her effort to show love, has unwittingly created a monster that is now beyond her control. That is, until he runs into the brick walls of the law and the court system.

How does this happen? Against this backdrop of dozens of similar scenarios, it has become obvious to me that some mothers have sought to replace their absent spouse with the love for a child. But such a relationship is unbalanced. A parent may be absent from the home for a variety of reasons—separation, divorce, death, drugs, imprisonment, or birth out of wedlock. Whatever the reason, whether right or wrong, the custodial parent must never cede their parental power to a child under the guise of love. It is a true recipe for disaster that will require rebalancing the relationship for the long-term best interests of the child and parent.

A few years back, a mother appeared in court with twin sons, who were completely out of control. They were charged with criminal mischief and arson. Following their being denied privileges as a result of fighting in the home, they began to destroy their bedroom, throwing things around and damaging or breaking items and putting holes in the walls until law enforcement was called. These youth were only ten years old but had developed an attitude of invincibility as well as anger, bitterness, and jealousy toward each other. Because of the repeated fights with one another, the parents decided to separate, each taking one son so that they would not "kill each other." Amazingly, these youth, though young in age, appeared hardened as they stood before me in court. I had to take on a harder than usual persona as one stared at me as if he was not intimidated at all. Yet, unlike the parent, I did not tolerate the disrespect and in fact ended up locking up the one who tried to display the harder demeanor for a full twenty-one day stay. Counseling and other services were subsequently ordered by me and so far, from all indications, they have remained out of trouble. However, it took the strong intervention of the court in order to reverse the conduct of these twin brothers. Unfortunately, by the time they turned around, their parent's marriage had actually failed.

I have also noticed that even with relationships between siblings, single mothers often elevate the sons to a higher level than their daughters. The daughters are given responsibilities to care for the house, such as cooking, cleaning, and maintaining the home, while often the sons are let off the hook. Often, the guy's conduct is condoned, whether it is good or bad. Unfortunately, all too often, the conduct is bad. The daughters get the Cinderella treatment while the sons become the Prince Charming. However, there is usually no silver slipper for the daughter. The daughter is often chastised for small errors while the sons get away with everything. The sons hang out all times of night and if and when they come home, they expect the women in the house to serve them their dinner. They are being conditioned to treat women like servants. In their eyes, females within the house are supposed to do the cooking, washing, and cleaning. Outside of the house, this attitude fuels the belief that women are only good for sex, money, or whatever else they can be used for. These young men look for females who will treat them like their mother did. They will feign responsibility and look for the easy road of life. Often they will hang out on the street corners without any goal or direction in life, except to use people for their own personal benefit without regard for the feelings of others.

The street life becomes even more enticing as these young men look for the easy way to hustle money. Whether running drugs as a young teen, or controlling his own corner as he gets older, the inevitable result will be jail or death. Many times, these youth will come home and "break off a piece of money" to Momma. This will keep her on his side, but out of his business. Yet this conduct will eventually have its own set of consequences.

In their desire to raise their sons, some single mothers push their daughters away. Unfortunately, many of these daughters end up disavowing their mothers and saying they will never be like her. Sibling rivalry spills over into the court system with fighting between the siblings, sometimes even with weapons being used. Often the rift never heals, and later in adult life, the siblings continue their dislike for one another, even through the death of the parent and fight over the remaining estate that is left behind.

On another front, there is the mother who pampers her son into being a momma's boy. "Momma's boy" never does anything wrong. He does not have much responsibility at home. On the surface, he goes to school, exhibits good manners at home, and maybe even goes to church. Instead of hanging out on the street corner, he has learned to fly under the radar to avoid detection. He is the one who sneaks around with one or more girls and may occasionally or regularly engage in unprotected sex. When one of the females that he has been sleeping with comes up pregnant, his mother is shocked. "Not my son, not my baby! How did this happen?" When the girl or her parents step forward to talk to him about his responsibilities as a prospective father, his mother may go ballistic. She sees him as her boy, and can't imagine him having the responsibility of being a father. Sometimes the initial shock wears off and the mother encourages him to take care of his responsibilities as a young father. More often than not, the momma's boy's mother views the situation with the girlfriend along the lines of "I took care of my children without a father, she can do the same. She has parents to help her. I need my son to help me and that little hussy/skank/skeezer, can figure out her own situation. That little hoochie probably tricked my son, anyway. I bet that baby is not his. My son is a good boy."

All of the thoughts that the mother is thinking are inconsequential, so long as they remain within her mind. The problem arises when there is a confrontation between the two families. The girl and her family confront the boy, usually when he is with another girl. An argument erupts, a fight occurs, and somebody goes to jail. The court system becomes involved to deal with the delinquency charges. But now it also has to address child support, the restraining order, the paternity testing, the repeat violence, injunctions for protection from one family to another, and more.

Could this have all been avoided if mom recognized her limitations with raising a boy early on and sought the help of the absent father? What about the youth's uncles, the pastor or men at the church, the coach at school or some other male figure who would be willing to work with her to mentor the son during the difficult years of growing up? I suggest that seeking help early is the ticket to reducing the likelihood of this scenario. Secondly, pouring moral values into the child through venues such as church is helpful. However, day in and day out communication between parent and child carries the greatest influence. Do not allow your expectations to be low on the one hand or overexaggerated on the other. There are no perfect kids. Instead of perfection, it is more appropriate to raise morally strong, positive, productive children who can take care of themselves as adults.

As I grew up and learned how to drive work trucks, I learned about the "governors" which are put on trucks to keep them from exceeding the speed limits. In much the same way, humans in general and kids in particular, need governors to keep their conduct in check and avoid those things that get us in trouble. Parents play a unique role as governors for their children and have a duty to set limits on the child's conduct. As the child matures and is able to handle more responsibility, the parents can loosen the limits. However, never allow those limits to be compromised by giving the child the power to replace the space of an absent parent.

Parents should also be very cautious of talking bad about the absent parent. When a parent speaks against the absent parent by referring to him as a deadbeat dad, trifling, drug addict, womanizer, or any of the host of terms which one parent may say about the other, it plants negative seeds in the minds of the children. The younger the child is who experiences this fusillade of negativity, the greater the likelihood that the child will internalize these assaults as his own. It is important to remember that the child is a combination of both father and mother. When one parent talks bad about the other parent, the child is unconsciously picking up that "if my dad is bad, then I must be too, since I am a part of him." The same is true when dads talk negatively about mothers. Be mindful of this conduct, as it will deposit seeds of negativity in a child that can blossom into later problems or misconduct. Parents should never overlove a child due to the loss or absence of a spouse. The role of the parent is too precious and important for the success of the child to be compromised by getting the relationship out of focus. Children, particularly those who are being raised in a single parent home, need the discipline of parental authority in their lives. They need parent(s) to be parent(s), not their friend(s). Never get those roles twisted. They are clear and distinct.

Practical Tips

1. Parents should never say what their child will or will not do when he/she is out of their sight.

2. Parents should not treat children as their equals. They are children, not little adults.

3. While each child has a different personality, parents must not elevate one child over the other.

4. Single mothers will need help with raising boys and should seek out positive role models or mentors as soon as possible.

Chapter Thirteen:

Never Allow Children to Settle for Mediocrity

> *Parental acceptance of a child's refusal to attend school, complete and turn in homework, or misbehave in school is a sure ticket to disastrous, long-term consequences.*

C hildren are very malleable. The human body has the physical ability to grow and expand in size from a newborn infant into a maturing teenager. That alone is a miracle when one considers that a newborn weighs an average of six pounds, and in a period of fifteen to eighteen years, that child grows to average height of sixty-eight to seventy-six inches. It stands to reason that if the outer shell of the body can grow in such a fashion, so too can the inner core which reflects our personality and intellect.

The human brain is the most sophisticated organ of the body. It controls every movement, thought, idea, or action. If it has the ability to direct the body to grow physically, it also has the ability to grow mentally as well. Because the brain is capable of learning, the human being is capable of performing miraculous tasks. New inventions, strategies, and concepts are all the result of a creative mind overcoming daunting challenges.

Parents should never allow children to settle for mediocrity in their thoughts, words, or deeds. Parents know or should know their children better than anyone else. Children are the seed of their father. They were carried and born of their mother. They have been observed throughout their lives under a parental microscope. Parents should never allow a child to settle for anything less than their best. While no two children are exactly alike, there are significant similarities that remind us that every child can learn, even if they process the information differently.

Mediocrity is acceptable only to the mediocre.

All too often, I have witnessed parents make excuses for their children's negative attitude toward school. Children are permitted to watch television or play video games past midnight and into the wee hours of the mornings, sometimes with the parent's knowledge. But when the alarm goes off to wake-up the next morning, and the child doesn't want to get out of bed, he or she is often permitted to sleep in and miss school.

One can quickly see this is a recipe for falling behind in school. Once a child gets on the slippery slope of not attending school or not doing homework without parental consequences, it is not long before the child begins to take the path of least resistance everywhere in life. When an eight-year-old begins to dictate whether he wants to study or go to school, there is a problem brewing. If parent(s) permit this attitude to remain, there will be major problems ahead. Without intervention, the child will continue to do just enough to get by. Soon the child will become the tail that wags the dog.

A strong example of a parent's failure to control her household comes to mind. A single mother and her oldest son began appearing in front of me a few years back after the school system reported him as being truant. Of course, his truancy opened the door for other forms of trouble. The young man stayed up most of the night watching television or playing video games. When time for school rolled around, he refused to get up. He amassed an inordinate number of absences from school, at least sixty-five percent before the matter came to court. After he plead out to the shoplifting of (you guessed it) video games and striking his mother, I placed him on probation. One of the conditions required him to attend school on a regular basis, without tardies, absences, or behavior referrals. It wasn't long before he violated probation by not attending school. I put him in custody, not once, but several times in an effort to get his attention, but all to no avail. I finally sent him to a commitment program to serve out his juvenile sentence.

Not long after, the same conduct began to repeat itself with the younger brother not going to school. The same result occurred. Next up, the younger sister did the same thing, fighting her mother and refusing to go to school. I suppose you can say that she learned by watching her brothers get away with not going to school and not obeying their mother. The daughter also went to a short-term commitment program and after returning home, the mother surrendered her to foster care as she could not do anything with her. Since she has been in foster care, the child, now seventeen, is attending school and following the dictates of the court order. I recognized that the one common factor in each of the three cases was the mother's inability or unwillingness to push her children to succeed. Early on, the simple act of shutting off the television, taking away the video player, and demanding that they go to bed at a reasonable hour, thus resting each of them for school the next day, could have changed the outcome.

The two older boys, having dropped out of high school are now over eighteen, back home and continuing the same pattern of sleeping all day and staying up all night to play video games. Needless to say, their lives will be destined for mediocrity, as both lack motivation and neither has an education. An even younger daughter, who is now eleven, was also removed from the mother's care because the mother allowed a registered sex offender to move into the home. This child seems to be thriving with a non-relative.

Parental acceptance of a child's refusal to attend school or do homework, or to act out in school, is a sure ticket to disaster. Some psychologists will theorize that rebellion among tweens and teenagers is a common part of the adolescent hormonal upheaval. But left unchecked, the misconduct can manifest itself into more serious conduct causing the youth to end up in jail, strung out on drugs, or even dead. This is too high of a price to pay for behavior that could have been redirected had the parent acted earlier to check the conduct.

Parents also must be on guard against allowing the youth to manipulate them into believing that mediocrity is acceptable. A young lady appearing in court before me on delinquency charges involving defiant behavior directed toward her adopted mother actually tried to justify her conduct by telling me that she had been diagnosed with Opposition Defiance Disorder (ODD) and therefore she was supposed to act difficult. To which I replied, "I have a diagnostic label also. It is called J.U.D.G.E. and I will lock you up if I have to in order to treat your ODD." After several starts and stops, including a short-term commitment, she has graduated from high school and is now a dispatcher for law enforcement in a neighboring county. She still keeps in touch with me and actually thanks me for opening her eyes to her potential once she gave up the negative attitude. While I would like to take some of the credit for her turnaround, the truth is that her mother never gave up on her, nor gave into her negative attitude or misconduct. Today, the youth has become a beautiful young woman, who takes care of herself, holds a responsible job, pays taxes, and will soon have completed her bachelor's degree.

The difference between the two scenarios above boils down to whether parents believe mediocrity is an acceptable standard. The noted educator, Dr. Benjamin Mays, former president of Morehouse College and mentor to Dr. Martin Luther King, Jr., U.N. Ambassador Andrew Young, and thousands of other young African-American men often stated:

> The tragedy of life is often not in our failure, but rather in our complacency; not in our doing too much, but rather in our doing too little; not in our living above our ability, but rather in our living below our capacities. Whatever one touches, his aim should always be to leave that which he touches better than he found it.

I am a firm believer that children will rise to whatever standard the parents accept. While not all children learn by the same method, every child has the capacity to learn and to be productive. Give kids exposure to learning environments from the earliest time possible. Maintain the importance of education throughout their formative years and continue to closely monitor them throughout high school until they lock into their own independent mindset and see the necessity of doing well in school as the precursor to a productive life. Never accept a one-dimensional child, such as emphasizing sports or physical beauty to the detriment of their studies. You will be pleasantly surprised to learn that the extra-curricular activities can serve as a motivator to encourage youth to pursue their studies. I have seen it work repeatedly, where a parent conditions good grades as a requirement for kids to participate in sports, beauty pageants, or the like. This is not a novel idea. Try it.

Practical Tips

1. Encourage children to do their best.

2. School attendance is not optional, it is mandatory.

3. Parents' acceptance of a child's refusal to attend school or do schoolwork is a recipe for long-term adult failure.

4. Parents should never give up on a child's performance, even when they receive a challenging personality diagnosis.

Chapter Fourteen:

Encourage Rather Than Criticize Your Child

W e are a talking society. People are constantly talking about everything from the weather and sports, to politics and the economy. The First Amendment to the U.S. Constitution promises each citizen the right to free speech, whether orally or in writing. Talking is the most important thing that Americans do. But with everyone talking, what is truly being said to our children?

> *A parent's faith in their child will push them to achieve more than anything or anyone else.*

Many from my generation remember the 1960s television character, Geraldine Jones, who was made famous by comedian Flip Wilson. Dressed in a wig, a mini-skirt, and high heels, Geraldine often used the phrase, "What you see is what you get, baby" which went on to become a staple phrase in the American vocabulary. I have come to learn that it is not what you *see* that you get—but instead it is what you *say* that you get.

One of my favorite scriptures, Mark 11:24, states that if "we believe the things we *say*, we will have what we *say*." History is replete with those who said they would be victorious and then went out and won. They became celebrated as heroes. Whether we talk about world-renowned boxer, Muhammad "The Greatest" Ali who proclaimed he would defeat Smokin' Joe Frazier, or Joe Namath's leading of the New York Jets to improbable victory over the Baltimore Colts in Super Bowl IV, or President Barrack Obama's victory over Senator John McCain in the 2008 election, each of them "received" what they *said* they would do.

Children need to be taught from infancy to have a positive mindset. When parents set a high standard for their children over a long period of time, children will usually rise up to the level of the expectation. When a parent says, "You can climb the backyard tree or the giant sliding board," you can bet your last dollar that the child will accomplish that feat. Parental faith in a child can accomplish wonders. Parental encouragement is more important than parental criticism. When we speak positive about our children, the children will learn to do the same. They will take on challenges instead of being intimidated by the lurid thoughts of fear. They will speak with confidence and not be intimidated. In the words of my mother, "You can catch a lot more flies with honey than vinegar."

Criticism on the other hand steals dreams. When a parent continually tells a child that he or she will never be anything, that he or she is stupid, worthless, lazy, and good for nothing, is it any wonder that they end up the way they are depicted? They hear the negative words and internalize those voices. Those negative "can't do" voices often drown out the still, quiet voice that says, "Yes, you can."

To reverse this degenerative disease of negativity that has crept into our society, it is critical that parents speak life into their children through positive words of encouragement. This is a potent way of turning our nation around from the "No, we can't" into the belief that "Yes, we can." As we know from experience, either way the utterance is correct.

All too often, I have youth appearing before me, proudly stating that their grades are okay. That usually translates into a C or D average. In the minds of these youth, those grades are enough to get by. My response is usually something to the effect that a C is nothing to brag about, unless it truly was your best. The usual response is that it was not their best. Amazingly, the parents often stand by and seem to go along with the kid's notion that getting Cs and Ds are perfectly acceptable. Parents should never accept a child's subpar performance unless it truly is their best. How does one instill a standard of excellence in a child, instead of mediocrity? It all starts with the expectations that you set for your child.

Building a Child's Faith to Succeed

I have spoken to many schools and youth groups over the years, and I often use personal parables to garner their attention and to encourage young people. One such example is as follows: Diamonds are considered to be the most valuable mineral on planet Earth. Diamonds, which are clear in color, are formed from black coal over a long period of time. Black coal also is used to heat furnaces and even backyard grills. Yet, what is the difference between a piece of black coal that is consumed in a furnace and the coal that has become the most valuable mineral on the planet? It is the ability of the coal to withstand pressure. The coal that becomes a diamond is transformed through enormous amounts of pressure over a long period of time, while the less valuable piece of coal is used to heat furnaces. One is celebrated, while one is consumed.

Children are like coal. Without proper discipline, some will be cast aside and consumed by the furnaces of this world. Others will be transformed by the process and become extremely valuable to the human race and the planet. It is the parents' influence that is the major factor for deciding whether a child will end up as a piece of charred coal or as a diamond, the most precious stone on the planet.

From the time of infancy, parents should adopt a "yes, you can, yes, you will" motto. For example, instead of parents fearing that the baby will fall when he starts to walk, hold the child's hand and help him to get back up when he falls. The same is true as he or she matures during the different stages of growth and development. Expose the child to books, the outdoors, and positive messages posted on their bedroom walls, on notes inside their lunch boxes, or in cards and letters to remind them that they are special and that you believe in them. Find ways to constantly reinforce a positive message to your child.

Do not allow the child to become addicted to television or video games. Television is not and should never be used as a babysitter. Too many young people find it easier to live in the fantasy make-believe world of television, even using such values as the way they view themselves and interact with others. Cut the television off during the school week and limit their viewing on the weekend. Monitor the program content at all times and never be afraid to cut the television off in order to protect the minds of your children. My, what a novel idea!

As children grow, keep the communication lines open, so that you always know what is going on in their lives. Keep the children talking to you, so that you can remain abreast of the things they are experiencing and the people with whom they are interacting. When they receive negative messages that threaten to blunt their progress, you are positioned to reenergize their faith in themselves.

Monitor Technology Used by the Child

Keep the bedroom door open, except when the child is changing clothing. This allows parents to monitor the child's computer activities and keep them on track to engage in positive conduct. Keep up-to-date with their activities, friends, and technology. MySpace, Facebook, Twitter, and cell phones are great tools, but they need to be monitored. Recently, a fourteen-year-old girl's cell phone came into the possession of my court bailiff after the phone repeatedly rang aloud during a court session. As he flipped the phone open, a nude photo of the young lady appeared. Shocked, he began to scroll through the phone and to his surprise, she had numerous nude photos of herself in multiple positions, which she apparently had been sending out in text messages to her friends as a joke.

The phone was turned over to her mother, who was totally embarrassed by the child's activities and promised to end her phone privileges. The child did not have a clue that once the text message was sent out, it could be forwarded hundreds, if not thousands of times to others. The pictures could wind up in the hands of unexpected and unsavory individuals, even sexual predators whose motives could create dangerous consequences for the unsuspecting child. The teen did not have a clue that her photos could attract such wrong type of attention. To her, it was only a joke. The mother did not realize that the child was engaging in this conduct.

The teens refer to this conduct as *sexting*, which to them is harmless. Yet there have recently been several cases where the purported innocent conduct is now resulting in criminal charges for the ones who are sending the messages. The consequences of this so-called innocent *sexting* or transmission of nude or semi-nude photos has caused some youth or young adults to be prosecuted and labeled as sex offenders. In light of recent federal and state law changes, the sex offender label can now follow the child into adulthood. The further impact of this conduct is that once an individual is labeled as a sex offender, he will not be allowed around children, thus blocking potential careers in education, law enforcement, and a number of other professions, all because of this purported innocent conduct.

The person depicted in the photos risks prosecution for the initial transmission of the pictures. They also run the risk of public embarrassment when the photos surface, as they always do, usually at a most inopportune moment. Renowned actress, Vanessa Williams, lost her Ms. America title after provocative nude photos taken before she became famous were published in the national media. Several other celebrities have come under public embarrassment after their nude photos or other embarrassing information has been exposed have emerged. Most recently, Detroit Mayor Kwame Kilpatrick and renowned professional golfer, Tiger Woods have fallen from grace when embarrassing text messages have been exposed to the general public.

A young Pinellas County, Florida teacher was arrested and prosecuted for sending her nude photos to a fifteen-year-old former male student. She thought her conduct was just for fun and made her cool with the students. She was arrested and her booking photo was displayed by media throughout central Florida and beyond. She also lost her job and for a period of time lost custody of her two young children. Prosecution, embarrassment, and loss of career opportunities are too high of a price to pay for *sexting* or other similar actions. Parents must educate their children to the consequences of this inappropriate conduct.

An interesting thing that has occurred with the development of technology has been the growth of an entirely new vocabulary. Those who regularly send and receive instant messages by computer or text messages via cell phones, use a unique shorthand lingo. Kids are therefore able to send and receive encrypted messages right under their parent's noses, even while the parents are standing over their shoulders. There are hundreds of these ever-changing codes. An abbreviated version of some of these acronyms will give you an idea of just why you need to be knowledgeable about your kid's communication activities.

BMA	Bite my a*s
CU	See you
DDSOS	Different day same old sh*t
DIS	Did I say
GTR	Got to run
POTS	Parents over the shoulder (My parents are watching, I can't really talk)
P911	My parents are in the room (either drop the subject or watch the language)
ROTFLMAO	Rolling on the floor laughing my a*s off
QT	Cutie or Cutie Pie
SOTR	Sex on the run
WMFS	Wanna meet for sex?

These are just a few samples of the terms that are used to communicate among teens via electronic technology. By no means are these all the terms. And to further complicate things, the terms are subject to change at any given time. Parents may want to go online to look at sources such as Wikipedia, Google, or Ask.com in an effort to keep up with what the teens are talking about and to see the current codes they are using.

Practical Tips

1. Parental faith in a child will encourage success even where the child's talents are limited.

2. Parents should never accept a child's subpar performance in school, conduct, or performance, unless it is truly their best.

3. Parents should stay abreast of the child's technological gadgets to make sure they are not being used inappropriately.

4. Parents should familiarize themselves with the terminology used by kids in order to thwart any negative activities that they may be planning.

Chapter Fifteen:

Just Because Everybody Else is doing "It" Is Not an Excuse for Your Child to Do So

Never let a child justify bad conduct.

One of the main excuses that children use when they appear in court on delinquency charges is that "I was hanging out with the wrong people." These so-called wrong people never show up in court with the accused to say that they are responsible for the misconduct. The accused is on his or her own, except for the parent who is there for support. No matter how many times the parent has yelled at, pleaded with, or begged the child, ending up behind bars is usually a significant wake-up call that was long overdue. For some, a short stay is sufficient, while for others, a more long-term commitment is necessary. In either case, the detention is the result of behavior that started because the child chose to imitate the conduct of their negative peers. They mistakenly believe that the conduct is cool because "everybody else" gets to hang out late, curses at their parents, steals from the store, or is using drugs.

Today's youth are under tremendous peer pressure. Many feel they need to emulate the urban dress styles shown on television in order to be cool. Their perception of themselves is usually premised upon whether they fit in with the cool kids or not. Many times, particularly where the child is struggling with self-esteem issues, the pressure to fit in with a certain crowd to which the child is drawn can be overwhelming. Clothing and dress styles are one thing. Behavior and conduct can be even more radical. Taken to the extreme, this "in crowd" will pursue the child to become a member of their clique, crew, or gang. In order to get in or be initiated, the new kid will have to do what the others have done or are doing. If that is wearing a certain fashion, getting high, sexing someone else, shoplifting, breaking into a car or house, or any of the host of misdeeds, depending on how bad the child wants to fit in, they will follow through. Kids will even get with other similar kids and form their own groups. Gothic dress styles or low riding pants and dreads are symbolic of kids' efforts to fit into a certain street image. One subset of kids who came to court for egging houses and battering neighborhood mailboxes and other criminal mischief, called themselves the Lost Stolen Minds. Does that suggest the fact that they were acting out and certainly not thinking about the consequences of their conduct?

While the tug of negativity is always present, especially for teens, it is important for parents to counter the negative peer pressure with their own version of positive image building. As a parent, you have a head start. From the time the child is born, a parent's positive influence carries more weight than that of anyone else because parents spend more time with the child than anyone else. Use this time wisely to build strong self-confidence in the child. Certainly, as the child moves out into the school setting, he or she will be exposed to other images that may be different from those he or she is accustomed to at home. However, when the child has been made to consistently feel good about him or herself, that image, coupled with some other commonsense ideas will prevail.

Additionally, it is very important to monitor your children's friends, closely. Trust your instincts. If your gut feeling is that the companions the child is hanging with are not good for him or her, chances are that you are correct. The earlier that the parent is involved in promoting a positive environment for the child, the greater the influence the parent will have on the type of friends the child will select. While not promoting the idea of being snobs, parents need to use wisdom in helping their children to select the right type of friends. From the time of early childhood, invite their friends to your home. Create a controlled environment, but do not become so overbearing that the children will not want to be in your presence. You can influence or control your environment, whereas you lack the ability to do the same for someone else's home.

Get kids involved early in structured community activities. These types of adult supervised activities can include athletic teams, dance, swimming, boy or girl scouting, boys or girls clubs, church youth groups, community organizations, and more. In getting kids involved with positive activities, the youth's relationships are arranged or rearranged so that their ideas, interests, and desires also change. By promoting teamwork, discipline, individual effort, hard work, accomplishment, and success, kids can be redirected from the negative ideas of gang activities such as stealing cars, burglarizing homes, doing drugs, and engaging in illicit sex due to the absence of adult supervision into a totally different mindset.

Parents who work with other parents in developing positive encounters for their children multiply the likelihood of success for all of the youth involved. As the African proverb says, "It takes an entire village to raise a child." When parents are drawn together to work on creating positive environments for children, the benefit far outlasts their own children. Collective efforts are major secret weapons in defeating the forces of negativity that are perilously seeking after our children. Just because everybody else is doing it is not a reason for your child to do so, unless it is doing something good.

Practical Tips

1. Monitor your child's friends. Never be afraid to trust your instincts.

2. Check out your child's friends and the friends' parents by inviting them to a controlled setting, such as a backyard cookout. This will help you get to know their friends and parents and help you to determine their suitability.

3. Help your child to develop a strong sense of personal identity so that he will not be overpowered by the force of day-to-day peer pressures.

Chapter Sixteen:

A Personal Success Plan for Your Child's Future

> *If you don't know where you are going, any road will take you there. Ancient Chinese Proverb*

Throughout this book, I have attempted to share the benefits of my experience and the wisdom of the ages, often referred to as common sense. One of the major tools that I have developed for the use of young people appearing in front of me I refer to as a "Personal Success Plan." The Personal Success Plan is designed to focus the youth's attention upon answering the proverbial question, "What do I want to be when I grow up?" Many young people have yet to set a career goal, even if it later changes. They seem to be clueless as to what is necessary in order for them to have a successful career. They have been led to believe that they can do whatever they like so long as they are less than eighteen years old. And they have been wrongly told that their juvenile records do not follow them into adulthood. This is painful misinformation. While juvenile court records are generally not open to the public, in an era of internet technology, there are many ways that one's delinquent conduct gets revealed. For example, certain enumerated felony juvenile crimes are reported in the press and may be counted in the score sheet calculations when that individual is later being sentenced for adult crimes. Where a youth's conduct makes local headlines, it only takes a Google search of an individual's name to reveal news articles that have appeared.

They have been told that they can run drugs, burglarize cars, and spend a few days in detention and, after they turn eighteen, they will get a clean adult record to start all over again. This could not be further from the truth. For example, many youth are painfully shocked to find out that they can be turned down by the military because of their juvenile delinquency record. The military can obtain access to juvenile records in order to determine whether to accept an individual into the service. One can readily understand the importance of such information in determining various levels of security clearances, weapons use, and access to technology. The same can be said for law enforcement credentialing. Certain government benefits can be denied based on criminal records. Admission to college or financial aid can be denied or turned down based on a juvenile delinquency history.

Many youth will drop out of high school once they accumulate significant absences as a result of being in and out of the detention center. They can fall so far behind in their grade levels that they end up older than their classmates and physically taller than the other children in their class. Often they become too embarrassed to even show up for school.

In many of the messages I have given over the years, I remind my listeners, particularly young people, of their unique importance to our society and the world in which we live: "Look around your classroom, your church, or even your own home. Is there anyone you see who looks exactly like you? We know the answer to that; none of us are exactly alike. Even identical twins have something which makes them different. Everyone is unique as proven by fingerprints or DNA. Could it be that God intended you to be special and to use your own unique talents or gifts to change the world around you? That's why any failure to maximize your skills or gifts will deprive the world of something special that only you could have accomplished."

The Personal Success Plan was developed in order to force youth to take a serious examination of their future. They are required to identify their goals in several key areas of life. For example, if a student in high school wants to be a lawyer, he or she should research the requirements to become a lawyer, such as graduate from college, take the LSAT exam, complete three years of law school, and maintain good citizenship in order to pass the background check that will be required before admission to the bar. If the desire is to be a firefighter, he or she must graduate high school, complete a two-year degree at the community college, and pass a state certification examination and background check showing that he or she is free of felony criminal convictions.

To become a nurse, he or she will have to obtain a two-year degree for certification as an LPN or Licensed Practical Nurse, or bachelor's degree plus state examination in order to become an RN or Registered Nurse, and complete a background check. If a youth wants to become a medical doctor, he or she will need to obtain a solid background in science and math, graduate from a four-year college, be accepted and complete medical school and a one- to two-year residency, pass the medical boards and a background check. If a youth wants a career in the military, he or she will need to remain drug, alcohol, and conviction free plus complete high school or obtain a GED or general equivalency degree in order to become an enlisted soldier. If he wants to be an officer, he will need to complete a four-year college degree program. Whatever the field of endeavor selected by the youth, he or she is required to research the requirements for the job and to identify at least one person who is successful in that occupation. The earlier that parents get their youth to begin thinking about his or her future, the sooner that accountability and responsibility will emerge.

Creating a Personal Success Plan

A Personal Success Plan includes the following:

1. My Personal Goals

   What do I enjoy doing?

   What am I good at?

   What gifts and talents do I have?

   What comes easy for me but would be more difficult for others?

   Answer these questions and you are well on the way to identifying your personal goals. Once you identify your personal goals, then you can explore your vocational goals.

2. My Vocational Goals

   What is my ideal job, profession, business, or career? Talk to someone in that field or research the area through the Internet to determine what you need to do in order to achieve your dream job or career. Is a professional license needed? If I get in trouble with the law, will I be disqualified from getting a license to practice my vocation?

3. My Educational Goals

    Knowledge is important. What must I do to get the education needed to accomplish my goals, such as completing high school, college, vocational, or other specialized area of study?

4. My Financial Goals

    What level of financial security do I want to have? How much will it take in order to acquire a home, a car, or pay for a college education? What about taking vacations with my family, saving money for emergencies or special projects, developing my own business, paying for health insurance, acquiring financial freedom, and saving for early retirement?

    Research the general costs of the above items to get an idea of the income level it will take to accomplish your desired goals. Talk to someone who can mentor you to plan and accomplish your goals.

5. My Recreational Goals

    What fun things do I enjoy doing? How do these activities fit into my long-term life goals? Will my athletic skills help me to go to college? What do I need to do to open doors of opportunity based on my skills and preferences? What will motivate me to contribute to improving society?

6. My Selection of Friends Goals

    What type of friends do I hang out with? Do they want the same things that I do? Are they planning to go to college or join the military? Do they encourage me to do the right thing at all times? Do they stand by me when I encounter difficulties?

7. My Family Goals

   What will my family look like? Will I marry, and if so, when? What should I look for in a mate? Do I want to have children and if so, when and how many?

8. My Health and Fitness Goals

   What do I need to do to remain healthy, to avoid illegal drugs and alcohol addictions, maintain proper weight, and live a long and productive life? Should I talk to a counselor, therapist, or someone to better understand my strengths and weaknesses? Am I a well-rounded person? What role does regular exercise play in living a healthy life?

9. My Spiritual Goals

   What are my spiritual goals and what must I do to accomplish these? Will I practice my faith by attending church and being involved in church activities? Will I want to attend a college that teaches information from the scriptures and helps me to live a value-centered, moral life? What type of church will I attend? How often will I attend? What will be my level of involvement? Will I study consistently beyond what is discussed in church, such as through a personal bible study program? How do I carry out my spiritual beliefs on a daily basis?

10. Other Areas

Are there some special areas of my life that I need
to address that are not included above?

This plan will become your personal road map
to lead you from teen years into adulthood and
beyond.

Parents will benefit by completing a model plan
for themselves as well.

Each of the above goals should be thoroughly explored. The
entire document should be approximately five to seven typed,
double-spaced, and error-free pages. Cite books, articles, or
periodicals used in developing this plan. Invest quality time in
putting this Personal Success Plan together; it will become an
excellent road map for your life. Keep a copy for yourself and
review this plan on a regular basis to keep your goals at the
forefront of your life. Work to make your dreams come true.

The Personal Success Plan is flexible and designed to benefit
anyone who takes the time to put it together and to follow
through with its implementation. Parents who work with their
children to create their plan for success will spend less time dealing
with law enforcement and the courts, as their youth seriously
begin to understand the roadmap for accomplishing their life
goals. When youth realize that in order to pursue certain careers,
including college or military, felony convictions as a juvenile can
quickly sideline such plans, many will often begin to reexamine
their conduct. I have had numerous youth come back and ask me
to set aside convictions so that they can get into the military. The
problem is that such requests are impractical and are too little,

too late. Certain academic scholarships are not available to youth who have juvenile felony convictions. Even numerous juvenile misdemeanor convictions can take their toll on a youth's future. While they may ultimately be admitted to college, the effort to get in may be magnified by the need to explain one's conduct. Entrusting your admission to college in the hope and expectation that the admissions officer has a heart and is willing to offer the youth a second chance is extremely risky.

When young people have lengthy juvenile records, employers have the right to question if they can trust the youth with company property, vehicles, computers, the cash register, or even keys to the office. Often, the process of having to sit down and put together a Personal Success Plan serves as a wake-up call for youth, who suddenly realize that they must begin to make much better choices in order to avoid derailing their lives even before they get started. The good part about getting a handle on the situation early is that the youth can turn things around if they are serious about doing so.

As the Personal Success Plan is taken in conjunction with each of the other suggestions discussed, parents and children will not spend time worrying about avoiding the negatives, but focusing on the positives. Young people who have a dream that they believe is attainable are less likely to get into trouble than those who have no dreams to pursue. The great educator and Morehouse College president emeritus, Dr. Benjamin Mays, often reminded his students, "The tragedy of life doesn't lie in not reaching your goals. The tragedy lies in having no goal to reach. It isn't a calamity to die with dreams unfulfilled, but it is a calamity not to dream. It is not a disaster to be unable to capture your ideal, but it is a disaster to have no ideal to capture. It is not a disgrace not to reach the stars, but is a disgrace to have no stars to reach for. Not failure, but low aim is sin."

One of the main reasons that so many of our youth end up behind bars as teens and later in their adult lives is because they have lost their sense of purpose. Parents who help them to acquire their sense of purpose through these described exercises will not have to worry about the failures that lead to imprisonment.

In doing so, parents will have accomplished the goal of this book, *How To Keep Your Child from Going to Jail.* While recognizing there are no absolute guarantees in this life, the ideas in this book have worked and are still working. They have been proven over many generations and yes, even in my own life, through my children and many others who I have mentored. They represent the wisdom for our children's future. Follow these ideas, and build a strong relationship and future for your child.

Practical Tips

1. As children begin to grow into adolescence, parents should begin to help them develop a Personal Success Plan. By the time a child is fourteen to fifteen years old their future ideas for themselves are beginning to crystallize. Use this exercise to not only create goals, but mold conduct.

2. Help children to identify their goals, but don't bully them to your goals.

3. Build your own Personal Success Plan along with your child. Each of us can stand to make some improvements in our lives from time to time.

Chapter Seventeen:

Closing Arguments

Not a day goes by when the media does not report that juvenile crime has occurred. If we only look at these media reports, one could surmise that there is little hope for our future. However, the reality is that the vast majority of young people are doing positive things and not getting into trouble. While there are too many youth who are dropping out of school, each one who we are able to save is a plus for the positive side of the ledger. But neither the courts, nor the school system can do it alone. Parents are the critical factor in reducing delinquency and setting children up for a positive future. Developing a strategy to keep a child on track is not something that can wait until the child is standing in front of a judge. The best approach is to begin a strategy at the time the child is born.

With our education system focusing on developing minimum standards that are evaluated by taking standardized tests, less and less focus has been placed on areas such as life skills, self-esteem, personal finances, and relationship building. Yet these intangible areas are critical to long-term success for individuals and our society as a whole. Parenting is both a privilege and a responsibility of bringing another human being to maturity. In the process, parents have a corresponding duty to use those same human gifts and strategies to increase the probability that their children's efforts will be successful.

My journey to this point in life is a direct result of the influences of many teachers and mentors. Not all of those lessons were in formal classrooms. Yet those life lessons were no less important to my success. Any of us could have gotten off course—myself included—and ended up in worse predicaments. That is why the information contained in this book is so important. It is time to open the eyes of parents and children to those challenges that can steer any unsuspecting individual off course and lead them into a dead end. One of my young parents that I supervise in Family Drug Court recently submitted the following poem to me as a testimony of turning her life around. It is used here with her permission to encourage others.

> Not long ago, I was traveling on this dark road.
> I went down the wrong way and almost lost my soul.
> I wasn't alone on this road, many were there,
> Wandering around lost and in despair.
> Living for today, not knowing what tomorrow holds,
> Just lost and confused not caring about my soul.
> There were many sleepless nights,
> When I wanted to just give up the fight,
> But something from within wouldn't let me give in.
> Even though my strength was gone
> And I felt so all alone.
> I began to think, where did I go wrong?

I wasn't raised this way, what would mama say,
If she could see me this way?
I knew something had to happen,
It had to happen fast, I was slipping away like sand in an
    hourglass.
Where would I start, what would I do?
Who could help me? If only I knew.
I slept through the day, and lay awake at night,
Waiting, when the time occurred to take up that flight
From the one that was going nowhere,
The same evil one which got me into this despair.
If only I could turn back the hands of time.
This mess would have never been mine,
O what choices I made.
I remember looking at myself, thinking where did the time go?
How did I get here?
Who's that looking back at me with a blank stare?
I lost all hope, my dreams were dashed,
Happiness was far away, who could imagine that?
I could have lost my mind, even my life, but God spared me,
Just one more time.
I thought about my kids, wondering would I be around to
    see them live.
The rate I was going, it wouldn't be long,
Before death came to carry me home.
I remember thinking I wanted to live, I didn't want to die.
If God could spare me, I swear I'll change my life.
He did just that and far more, He wiped away my sins and
    told me,
Hey, no more.
He welcomed me with opened arms,

And to my surprise,
He said my child,
I'm glad you came home.

Submitted by E F.

It is my hope that this work is indeed opening the eyes of parents and children alike. I have learned over the years that in spite of life's barriers, success is no longer limited to race, gender, or culture. Millions of people throughout our country are successful in their lives, in spite of the obstacles they have encountered. They are successful because they made a choice to be successful. We can no longer paint a picture of despair and say what one cannot do with his or her life. President Barack Obama, my hero, and countless others have shown us that success starts with a choice. And with faith, the right attitude, hard work, and determination, one can succeed against the odds. The sooner that we instill the idea of success in the minds of our young people, the sooner they will turn from a mindset of rebellion and failure. Parents have the primary duty to sow these seeds of success into the next generation.

Becoming a parent, whether biological, adoptive, or through mentoring, means being willing to make sacrifices for your children. Give your children a good start by helping them to develop a spiritual foundation. Talk to and not at your kids so that they will be able to hear. Parents, you are in charge of your house and never give that leadership or responsibility away to your child. Spend time with your kids. Such time spent is more precious than the total of all the money that you make and spend. Don't make excuses for the misbehavior of your child. To do so only extends the time and difficulty of reigning them back into the fold. Don't overprotect your children to the point where they are afraid to make decisions or leave the nest when the time comes for them to do so.

Keep a close eye on the friends they make and keep. Show me the friends they associate with and I will show you their future. Set and keep *your* rules of conduct for the house. Don't overlove a child to fill the gap of an absent spouse. By overlooking his misconduct, you are setting him or her up for problems and consequences later in life. Never allow a child to settle for mediocrity. Encourage, more than criticize your child. Just because everybody else is doing it, is not an excuse for your child to follow, especially if it is wrong. Where is the long-term profit in wrong doing? Help develop a Personal Success Plan, for you and your child's future. In the process of following this advice, I have no doubt that you will be successful in keeping your child from going to jail. Even more important, you will help them to become successful adults. May God bless you on the journey.

Hubert L. Grimes

Resources

The Holy Bible, King James Version

"Personality Synopsis," from Erik Erikson's Ego Psychology, http://allpsych.com/personality synopsis/Erikson/html.

Kay, Olivia. "Why Verbal Abuse Can be Just as Damaging As Physical Stress."www.helium.com/items

Florida Statutes (2009)

U.S. Department of Commerce. "U.S. Census Bureau News" www.census.gov/Press-Release/www/releases/archives/children/01/08

Office of Juvenile Justice Delinquency Prevention, U.S. Department of Justice, Statistical Briefing Book.http//ojdp.ncjrs.gov/ojstatbb/offenders

Webster's New College Dictionary, Houghton, Mifflin and Company: New York, 1995.

Mays, Dr. Benjamin E. Quotable Quotes of Benjamin E. Mays. Vantage Press: New York, 1995.

"Text messaging Lingo." http://answers, yahoo.com//questions/index.

Manufactured By: RR Donnelley
                    Momence, IL USA
                    July , 2010